THE ADOPTEE SURVIVAL GUIDE

Adoptees Share

Their Wisdom and Tools

Edited by Lynn Grubb

Cover Art by Carlynne Hershberger

The Adoptee Survival Guide

Adoptees Share Their Wisdom and Tools

An Anthology

Edited by Lynn Grubb

First Print Edition: 2015

ISBN-13: 978-1508544548

ISBN-10: 1508544549

Cover Art: Carlynne Hershberger

Please visit our Facebook page for comments and feedback

Praise for

The Adoptee Survival Guide

Adoptees Share Their Wisdom and Tools

2015

"This book is as much about thriving as it is surviving! These voices invite each of us to walk into the unknown, unheard, and under-valued sacred voice of the adoptee. Enter into a place of discovery, mystery, unlimited questions and a kaleidoscope of answers.

The stories here will challenge you, inspire you, cause you to reflect and perhaps even cry. That's okay – The Adoptee Survival Guide will enable you to see the forest through the trees!" – LeAnne Parsons, Adoptee, Certified Professional Coach, Speaker, and Radio Host.

* * *

"This survival guide is a buffet of thoughts and tidbits by various adopted people. Some were adopted as infants, some older. Each person's story is the story of one but this choir of voices gives the non-adopted parents and professionals out there a chance to listen and learn about some of the feelings, thoughts, frailties and fantasies of the adopted. Insight is a map to survival." – Dr. Joyce Maguire Pavao

"Humor is the highest defense mechanism. We were quick and early to learn whatever we needed in order to survive. We are survivors. We learned it from our birth parents and we learned it from our adoptive parents. We can laugh at ourselves. We can laugh at the world around us and we can play. We have the gift of play and fantasy because we have lived in a world of fantasy and not-knowing for oh, so long."

– Dr. Joyce Maguire Pavao as quoted in *Dear Wonderful You: Letters to Adopted & Fostered Youth*

TABLE OF CONTENTS

PART III: SURVIVING SEARCH AND REUNION

PART IV: SURVIVING REJECTION

PART V: SURVIVAL TOOLS

AFTERWORD

INTRODUCTION

by Lynn Grubb

The party-line within the mainstream adoption community says that adoption is a blessing and positive-only, so it may come as a surprise to some readers that many adoptees view being adopted as something to be survived. Due to the glamorization of adoption in the media and other factors, adoption is often not recognized as having *loss* at its root. In addition, it is often unacknowledged that the many issues adoptees face throughout their lives, could, in fact, be normal reactions to the original losses of biological kin, names, heritage, home state or country, language, medical history and identity.

The current awareness of post-adoption issues has been mostly the work of adult adoptees who speak out about their own experiences growing up adopted and the minority adoptive parents, therapists, social workers or other professionals who understand the deeper issues involved in being adopted.

This book came into creation as a result of my entrance into the on-line adoptee community. Many in these adoptee communities, like me, seek emotional support while navigating the labyrinth of adoption landmines. Some of the adopted members of this community are writers; however, many are just fellow travelers in search of information, lost family members, and wondering if there are others out there who feel like they do.

Some are managing the shock of being newly anointed into the group referred to as LDAs (Late Discovery Adoptees) having grown up believing they were the biological children of their parents and later learning that they were in fact, adopted.

"Who Am I?" seems to be the common theme amongst my fellow adoptees, along with concerns about discriminatory legal practices in the sealing of adoptees' original birth certificates (OBCs) and the observation that many outside the adoption community view us as "adopted children" who never grow up. Some of us have taken the plunge into genetic genealogy seeking answers and others have become open records advocates.

What each adoptee shares within these on-line communities is a need for perspective, advice and support on how to live this adopted life.

* * *

I started dabbling in writing beginning in 2005 while my daughter was an infant. My daughter's adoption was finalized that same year, triggering many painful post-adoption issues within me. I experienced a level of grief that surprised me. I was not only grieving for my daughter's loss of her mother (and our loss of a family member) but finally, at age 39, I was grieving the loss of the mother I never knew.

During that time period, my eleven-year-old son, Matt, the computer guru of the family, helped me to set up a Myspace profile. I began posting some of my adoption thoughts on Myspace while I began searching for my biological family and adjusting to life with a new baby.

Many laughed at me for taking part in Myspace as it was considered, at the time, to be a place for a generation much younger than myself. I embraced this new social media technology and connected, for the first time, with other adult adoptees who had either read my adoption blog posts at Myspace or in the forums of Adoption.com.

My entrance into the Facebook adult adoptee community was by way of Amanda H.L. Transue-Woolston and the Lost Daughters in 2011. I was invited by Amanda to write a guest post for Lost Daughters in regards to being an adoptee conceived in rape. I wrote under the pen name, "Jill" because it was all new and scary to me to put my story out there, and rape is such a hot button topic for readers. At the time I wrote my guest post, I had recently been told by my birth mother that I was conceived during a date rape. I needed support and I needed it quickly. I found it in connecting with other adoptees.

Support groups are not a new idea, however, support groups consisting of only adopted people and on-line were completely new to me at that time and a way to connect with adoptees in other states and countries from the comfort of my own couch.

The confidentiality of these adoptee-centric Facebook support groups provide safety in which the members of the group can disclose personal information in a supportive environment, without the perceived judgment by others who do not understand what living adoption feels like.

Some support groups may revolve around writing projects and others are centered on confidential discussions about the pitfalls of reunion, relationships with adoptive families, road blocks when searching for biological family in a closed adoption system, emotional triggers, and feelings of rejection and abandonment – that prior to joining a support group – many, including myself, weren't entirely sure were normal.

Just being a part of these support groups and knowing that one has complete acceptance – without having to explain – is a wonderful feeling, considering many of us don't come in contact with adoptees IRL (in real life) willing to talk about adoption issues face to face.

"Me too" is powerful and healing.

* * *

This survival guide is a sampling of many varied and honest adoptee voices. All of the contributing authors in this anthology (including the cover illustrator) are adopted. We have lived adoption and have some wisdom to share from our journeys. We may have different professions, hobbies, religions and live in different places, but we all share being adopted as our common thread.

The adoptees who penned these pages want to provide support, validation and encouragement to other adoptees, many of whom may not have a support group of their own, or may not even know another adoptee in their lives.

We acknowledge that adoption is not just a one-time event . . . it is a lifelong journey.

Our collective hope is that this book provides you the same comfort that we have received from the adoptee community. Now grab a cup of coffee or tea, a cozy blanket, and come along and walk with us in our shoes.

PART I: SURVIVING OUR ADOPTEDNESS

It's Not You, It's Adoption
(and the Many Triggers We Face Daily)

by Paige Adams Strickland

I've spent far too much time worrying and convinced that something is/was wrong with me. That's because I see things differently compared to my adoptive family. I feel things differently. I interpret everything in my environment in a way that often feels foreign and strange to them. Often their response indicates that I am wrong, and this saddens and frustrates me.

Am I incorrect? Am I crazy? Am I misinterpreting the message that I am wrong, so maybe I'm not wrong at all? How do I know for sure, and what makes other folks so secure about their perceptions?

I observe the special needs students I work with at school, and I've come to the conclusion that "adoptism" is a spectrum as well. Some adoptees could care less and never think of all the what-ifs and whys. Some never stop thinking about all the undisclosed details we may never know, the people we may never meet and how life might have turned out if…

Most of us are somewhere in the middle.

However, no matter where we land on this spectrum, we all respond uniquely to our environment. It's not always easy as adoptees to avoid certain triggers. Likewise, it's not always easy for non-adoptees to know what sets us off and makes us want to scream, cry, punch, throw or laugh at the absurdity, even when it's not appropriate to laugh. Among fellow adoptees, we can accidentally trigger one another, and it's very difficult to know what might happen to whom when.

Because of my "adoptism," it is a challenge to describe what makes me feel awkward, why I react the way I do. Even as a mature, logical and educated person who should know better, I hate feeling inferior, not measuring up to expectations or being left out. People don't mean to do these things to me, but I fall into patterns and situations where these things happen, because adoption put me there long ago.

Being adopted makes me read between the lines and question everything, especially change, grief and loss. If there really are stages, I think I am perpetually in the bargaining phase.

I don't take a lot of information at face value. I figure there is a story behind every message. There's a reason for everything, and I crave to know what it is. I detest having facts kept from me because someone thinks it's "for the best" or "for my own good". I'm a responsible adult. Let ME decide that, thank you very much.

I have learned to accept my "adoptism," and I usually cope well. I have my un-amended birth certificate, know my original name and have met my birth family. These advantages have taken away a lot of my former angst, but occasionally "adoptism" rears its ugly face and brings back feelings I try to ignore or purge, via writing, reading about fellow adoptees and doing exercise.

As each day passes I feel less adopted, though, and more like just me. I will always view life in my way, and not always the way my adoptive family sees it. I will process at my speed, have my own style and want to do things for myself in my own way. This is a good thing.

I love my life and feel grateful. Not just because parents came along and picked me out, but grateful for being alive. I am grateful, not just because I was given opportunities, but also because I had innate good sense and enough initiative to work hard for the things I wanted. I am grateful for knowing the people I know: family, friends, colleagues and the on-line people I've connected with. I am grateful for my work, my pets and my home.

I try every day to focus on these things more and less on the triggers of "adoptism". I will continue to push past feeling lesser and inferior to "regular-born" people. I will brush off the out-moded labels of "chosen" and "special". However, I won't stop asking questions, searching for info and accepting "No" for an answer. That's a learned way of life, and it's brought me satisfaction, closure and much affirmation when I've needed "Yes" the most.

We adoptees are survivors by nature. As the song says, we were "born this way".

A coping tool I use, as an adopted person, is by finding songs with lyrics that feed my soul and entertain my mind. Sometimes, but not always, the song may be directly related to the adoption triad concept, for example, Bruce Hornsby and the Range's The Valley Road. There are racial/class themes happening in the lyrics, but it can also be noted that the words to the tune reference a young woman's secretive, shameful, covered-up pregnancy and whisking the girl away to her sister's, but everybody knew what was really happening, much like what occurred during the Baby Scoop Era with unwed mothers-to-be.

On a personal level, this song reminds me of how my birth mother was sent to South Carolina to see her mother, while she was pregnant with me. She ended up having me in Ohio after all, but she left town for a few months just the same. She and my birth father also broke up around that time.

The Valley Road was a very popular song the summer I was doing my actual adoption search, and the music takes me back to that very exciting and emotional summer of navigating my way in busy, downtown traffic to the Hamilton County courthouse and library in search of the "Valley Roads" my first family must have followed before my time.

I also used to cope by hiding, lying and staying secretive about being adopted. The whole legal system was encouraging it when I was growing up, so faking became less frustrating until I learned that, in my case, my information was not forbidden after all. Once I was an independent adult, I began to cope by facing the truth and uncovering the past, or my past.

Now I cope by sharing my story and my thoughts about life as an adoptee. My real story was hidden for so long, and now I want it to survive in hopes that I can help other adoptees feel less alone and out of the loop.

I still appreciate and enjoy shows and songs that have adoption and adoptees as themes, (or some closely-related idea). I love on puppies and kitties in places like PetSmart and do my part for homeless pets.

Most of all, I thank the Universe every day for being healthy enough to have had my two children and the means and support to raise them successfully.

I am grateful for the opportunities provided via my adoptive family, which have educated and enriched my world, so that I can parent my daughters with enthusiasm and affection.

Because of the Long Valley Road my first family traveled, I was Born to Be Alive, and finally found them Somewhere Out There because I had Heart and Soul. Now, We are Family!

Paige Adams Strickland is an Ohio adoptee, teacher and writer. She is married with two daughters. She's been in successful reunions with her birth family for a long time. Paige is the author of *Akin To The Truth: A Memoir of Adoption and Identity*, about growing up with shame and secrets during the Baby Scoop Era and how it felt to be an adopted child and young adult.

Birth Day

by Wendy Barkett

"Be who you are in every situation" – Michael Johnson

As a phrase, "Happy Birthday" is a complete oxymoron for me. The two words in separate sentences work. In my 42 years, placing them together, has often not worked.

hap*py

Feeling pleasure: feeling or showing pleasure, contentment, or joy

Causing pleasure: causing or characterized by pleasure, contentment, or joy

Satisfied: feeling satisfied that something is right or has been done right

birth*day

Day somebody is born: the day on which somebody is born

Anniversary of day of birth: the day in each year is the anniversary of the day somebody was born

A week before my 42nd birthday I posted a status update on Facebook:

"Was going to post something totally obnoxious about my birth date being next week and then decided to spare y'all. Damn. I am getting old!"

The response to this update took me by surprise. It brought to the surface the reality of my feelings as well as stumped me in how to respond. I felt attacked for being ungrateful. One person said I should be happy I have family who does love me, for there are many children out there who are abused and neglected. I was told that I should be grateful for each year that I age. The list goes on.

I reached out to a dear friend and mentioned to her that this was why I must write about birthdays. When I told my husband what had been said, he simply shook his head and said, "They just don't get it." My feelings alone are not enough for so many around me. Simply allowing me to be sad on this day is not an option in their minds.

I was raised by two parents who had two biological sons. I was a fit for the family because they wanted a girl. I am the youngest of my siblings. There was never any doubt that I was loved. My goal here is not to touch on love, it's to touch a bit on the sadness that some, but not all, adoptees, may feel on their birthday. I can touch on it because I am an expert on birthday blues.

Sparing you the details of each birthday, I can, with a large smile tell you that I had many parties. While in kindergarten, my oldest brother entertained us all with a magic show. I can't recall if he was any good at magic but I can tell you, I was thrilled to be showing off my big brother. The fact that he decided to do the show for my day meant so much to me.

As a young child, grammar school age, I remember I did not like being the focus during the happy birthday song or the opening of gifts. What I enjoyed about my parties was being surrounded by my friends and seeing them having a good time. I did enjoy having a cake, as well as the chance to make my once-a-year wish, while blowing out the candles.

The wish was the same every year with a twist in the sequence of words or substituted words. I made the same wish until my 32nd birthday:

I wish to find my birth mother.

Each year on my birthday morning, I woke with hope. There were years where I would have never admitted to such dreamful hopes, but they were always there.

As a young child, I would hope that my birth mother would show up at our front door with a huge bundle of balloons. I could never see her face in these daydreams, as the balloons were in the way.

However, I would know it was her the instant I opened the door and she always got to stay for my party. As I became a teen, the hope turned to a phone call or a letter from her. Each time the phone rang, my body tensed with hope and then disappointment.

The balloons, the letter, and the phone call never came. I stayed silent about my wish because I knew the golden rule:

Don't tell anyone your birthday wish or it won't come true.

Many years I woke with hope that the day would go without any sadness and each year I was disappointed in myself for becoming sad. I always did my best to put on a happy face, especially for my parents. My mom put so much effort into each year's birthday event that I knew showing sadness might hurt her personally.

I had to smile for my friends as well. Making them think I was happy would in return help them to have a good time at my party. I wanted everyone to be happy. While I never could figure out how to make myself happy, I knew I was doing a decent job at faking it.

My teen years were less than desirable. Birthday parties ended at 14 years of age and I don't recall missing them. During the years of 14 through 18, my goal was to survive being a teen and to move out on my own.

On my 18th birthday, I called my mom at work and told her that my birth mother had called and wished me a happy birthday! She told me without hesitation that it was not my birth mother but rather someone playing an evil prank on me. I knew I had lied when I called her with my story but couldn't help but wonder what was so wrong with me? Why would my mom be so quick to say it never happened? My heart was broken.

Soon after turning 18, I moved out and walked a scary path into finding myself. The first step was to get a ride to the city where my adoption took place. It was a two and a half hour drive, but the mood on the way there was very upbeat.

I was going to the courthouse to get my adoption file and the thought of what I might find inside was overwhelming and exciting. It had never occurred to me in all the years I had visualized this – my 18th birthday – that I would be denied that file. The clerk let out a laugh when I asked her for it. I didn't allow her to see my tears.

When I was 21, I was married to a man in the military (we divorced when I was 23). I called my pediatrician from out of state. I told the secretary that I needed a copy of my medical files and explained to her that because I was now a military wife, I never knew who my doctor would be. And so she sent the file directly to me.

This was the first year for me to have any information at all. When I got the records, I studied them several times. There wasn't much in them that I was able to read as my physician really did have stereotypical doctor handwriting. I thought it said something about my birth mother being 23 years old and possibly on drugs. It also said I was born early, which I had already been told, but never knew it as fact.

Unless I saw something written in some sort of legal way, I would never believe much to be fact. I had, by this time, heard of other adoptees whose birth dates had been falsified. I was glad to see, at least by my doctor's records, that my birth date was indeed true.

My family continued to wish me a "Happy Birthday," especially my parents. They made sure to call and send me some sort of gift each year.

There were not any parties until I was in my mid 20's. At 27, I was now married to my current husband and best friend for a year. I was able to do more research about adoption records and laws online.

It was at 27 that I found out I could petition the court for what they call non-identifying information. I mailed in my forms as well as a check and then basically sat under the mailbox waiting for a reply.

No, I didn't really do that. I did, however, see the mailman coming each day and greeted him at the mailbox. When I saw the return address, I ran inside with my envelope. It felt thin. I had some idea what I could expect based on the experience of others which I had read about online.

It was a load of information on a typewritten form. It was this, my 27th year, when I found out the ages of my birth parents as well as what they looked like and their religions. I also found out that my birth mother was married but my birth father was not. I read it over and over and actually laughed. I was the product of some sort of affair? I felt a little bit of weight lifted from my back.

For my 30th birthday, my husband set up a surprise. He had called my boss and told her of his plans so I could have the time off for a surprise trip to Louisiana. He put so much effort into keeping the secret. He had no idea how it would backfire.

I was excited as we departed for our trip and even enjoyed the first day touring and checking out the different gift shops. He let me purchase the little trinkets I would later set on a shelf in remembrance of our trip.

The second day into our trip was my birthday. The blues set in and my husband spent several hours lying on the hotel bed watching me read a book he bought me as a gift. He never got upset with me. He never left the room. He just let me read my book, cover to cover, and then we headed out for dinner.

A week after we returned home, we were meeting his family for dinner at a popular theme restaurant. I stepped back into him as about ten people hollered out "Surprise!" to us. It was a surprise dinner – my first party since my 13th.

We spoke of the celebrations soon after getting home. I was desperate to figure out why I had felt so sad and appeared to some as so ungrateful. It was after our conversation that we made a new rule:

I am never again to go out of town ON my actual birth date.

While in Louisiana I could not help but wonder if I had missed the phone call I had for so many years wished for. It was my 30th after all and I thought if she was waiting for a special birthday to call on, surely this was it. I had lived at the same address for long enough that she should have been able to track me down. What if she had called and didn't leave a message? What if she decided not to call back? What if...

At one time along the way, I spoke to my parents about my distaste for my birthday. We tried to brainstorm via phone on how to make it better and one of them suggested celebrating the date they had brought me home. I shot down this idea immediately. I was brought home on my mother's birth date. For years, I felt guilt about taking away from her special day. I wasn't going to double hurt her by celebrating HER day as my own.

My 32nd birthday, I decided to go with faking it again. If I could plan a party and go over the top, maybe the happiness would sink in. I had an amazing cake and about 20 friends over. We even played pin the tail on the donkey. Goodie bags were given to each person or couple as they left. It was a great party, but the phone never rang with the unknown voice on the other end.

A month after my 32nd birthday, my world changed. It changes every day but this was the "before I knew/after I knew" change. A searcher had finally found my birth mother's name and then greeted me with the news of her death.

I had thought that by now, knowing part of my birth family history, my birthday would suddenly be worth celebrating and joyful. I had thought for so many years that the answer to my birthday blues would be birth family. Looking back, I know there was no way for me to know what might work or not work.

The first birthday after finding my truth was miserable. It was deep, dark, crawl back into bed miserable. It was the first year that I knew for sure that the phone would not ring with her voice on the other end, that a surprise birthday card from a woman I'd never met would not show up, and that the doorbell would not ring with a special woman behind balloons to greet me.

The pain of my loss, as well as the loss of my dream, was almost unbearable.

With my husband, I trudged on through the day. Honestly, I don't remember much from the entire month. I do remember that the pain was so strong that words were difficult to find.

My 40th birthday was greeted with a new kind of hope. It was a hope that I could enjoy the day. I went to bed early the night before my birthday. I was awoken by a friend who happened to stop by. She jumped on my bed and asked me to come outside to hang out with her. It was confusing, but I went out with her.

As we sat on my porch in the darkness, I saw a bundle of balloons floating up my driveway. It took my tired eyes a moment to focus and then the happiness set in with a bit of sadness. It was my birth sister with those balloons. She had known my birthday wish and while she couldn't bring my birth mother back, she gave me the next best thing. She surprised me for my birthday by flying in from out of town. The balloons were her way of showing a love that only she and I could possibly share.

The following day, my actual birthday, was supposed to be dinner with just the three of us. The plan was to eat at my favorite fondue restaurant for special occasions. As we walked in, I announced that I had to use the bathroom. Instead, I nearly peed myself as 40 people screamed out "Surprise!" I had no idea that this restaurant could provide a venue for so many people in one party.

My husband had, at some point in the year, decided to go all out and boy did he! He had invited friends from all time periods of my life!

The room was filled with happy memories. That night, all I felt was shock. There was not a moment of sadness. Banners filled the room with a photo of myself and the saying "Thank you for being a part of my journey".

My husband knows me on so many levels and knows that I refer to our lives as a journey. It was the most amazing birthday weekend ever, the first year I can recall having an actual "Happy Birthday!"

I still needed to explore why my birthday plagues me with such sadness and emptiness. This brings me back to my Facebook post.

Knowing that my birth mother is gone, still searching for the name of my birth father, being surrounded by family and friends who love and enjoy me – why do my birthdays still bring me to my knees with pain?

Tonight as I write this essay, the reason resurfaced. I had known the reason before, spoken of it even. Yet because it seems uncomfortable for so many, I bury it over and over. And for myself, it's time to just let it out.

To the very woman who created me, my birthday was a day of grief, darkness, sadness and shame. I will never hear the story of my birth or the story of loss from her mouth. I have, however, spoken to enough birth parents, in addition to knowing my birth mother well enough through my sister, to know this was not a good day.

My day coming onto this earth was filled with sadness and a lack of choice. I was brought into a world with tears of sadness rather than happiness – a product of an affair and a nervous breakdown, though I am not sure in which order.

I not only hurt for the mother I never got to meet, but for the innocent child that I once was. As a baby, I did not have the words to express my own sadness and needs.

I can only wonder if I reached out for my mother as I was taken away. I wonder if I cried for her and wondered why she never came.

Did she pass along some of her own sadness to me through my blood?

How shall I proceed into the future with my birthdays? With the power of truth. If I hurt, I have the right to feel those feelings. I have a right to cry on my birthday. I also have the right to celebrate.

It's my birthday. I get to choose.

Wendy Barkett writes of her personal struggles as well as triumphs in hopes that it will help adoptees feel less alone, and help non-adopted people to have a better understanding of some of her personal struggles. As her journey in a search for truth continues, she writes from the heart and without a filter.

Born in Ohio in 1972, she learned on her 18th birthday that the adoption laws in Ohio prohibited her from obtaining her original birth certificate. She spent years writing to anyone who would listen and was proud to be a part of the changed law in Ohio, which takes effect in March of 2015. She found her birth mother at a grave in 2004 and continues to search for her birth father.

Along the way, she continues to write in order to keep people aware of the challenges as well as the victories of her personal search. She is the author of *Shadows of a Dark-Alley Adoptee, an Adoptee's Search for Self.* She also has a website with a page listing all she has done over the years in her search in hopes that it will help others who are searching.

www.RememberDottye.com

Nobody Can Resist A Joyous Woman

by Rayne Wolfe

My birth certificate says I was born on a Thursday morning in San Francisco. But I know better now.

I grew up being told that I was special because I was adopted. My parents had to wait for years, fill out reams of paperwork, and pay lots of money to get me; I used to brag to my playmates.

"Your parents just got you. My parents had to search for me," I used to jeer at the mean boys on the playground who shouted "you're adopted!" like it was a curse.

My father was very intense in his mission to convince my adopted brother and I that being adopted was way better than just being born. Never mind that the book "The Bad Seed" was published in 1954, the year my older adopted brother turned four. Attitudes towards adoption hadn't improved much two years later, when I was born.

My father worried about social challenges ahead for his adopted kids. He taught us good manners, social dancing, and how to roll dice for drinks. He wanted us to always be proud of ourselves.

My mother was less supportive. She only lamely went along with my father's program of constant cheerleading for anything and everything even remotely tied to adoption.

I can put myself in my mother's shoes and imagine how strange it might be to know that you could have children but that your husband could not. In the days before fertility treatments, adoption was the only answer. That might explain why my mother was such a lousy mother in so many ways.

My earliest memories include "adopting" a new television set and adopting pets that fit perfectly into our family. Each night as my father tucked me into bed, he would whisper into my ear that I was his special girl.

My parent's divorce when I was ten-years-old meant that time with my father would be rare going forward. I can only imagine he left hoping his foundational work was strong: I was a special girl – even if I wasn't entirely sure why.

By my twenties, I had acquired all of my original adoption documents and after years of searching, was able to identify my birth mother, who turned out to be even more toxic than my very toxic adopted mother. Where my adoptive mother was cruel, my birth mother was cruel and crude. If my adopted mother shamed me for trying to get ahead in life, my birth mother, with her nearly indecipherable rural accent, made sure I felt like I was putting on airs.

I had been told by government agencies and my birth mother's extended family, that I was Scandinavian. But I always had doubts about my nationality. Having been conceived as a date rape, my birth mother said she knew little of the man's background. Yet, she was sure I was "half Norwegian and half Finnish." I accepted that as fact even though I often thought: Nobody's HALF this and HALF that.

I looked at my reflection in the mirror and imagined I could be a little Swedish. Or Polish. I can remember summers where I dressed like a girl from St. Tropez, in gauzy beach dresses and espadrilles, because I could be French. My identity grew to encompass all nationalities because, who knew what the heck could be in my gene pool?

I grew up in one of the most cosmopolitan cities in the world, attending summer camp in Chinatown, eating Italian food in North Beach, buying Sunday morning pastries in Russian bakeries. Even if it was only one per cent, I felt I could be Asian, Italian, or Russian.

Because I embraced the idea that I could be any nationality, I was interested in all nationalities. My identity was full of possibilities and I embraced the opportunity to create myself.

I decided I could also be like women I admired. I could be independent, like painter, Georgia O'Keefe (who also sewed her own clothes!) I could be adventurous like aviatrix and writer, Anne Morrow Lindbergh. I could become a cub reporter at age 40, a lifelong creative seamstress, or like my stepmother, whom I admired so much, just be "an appreciator" of so many cultural endeavors.

I had a long period through my thirties and forties that my philosophy about self-identity aligned with my thoughts on age. Chromosomes and birth dates mattered less to me than being honest and loving.

While my husband and I often lamented our lack of documented lineage, envying others whose grandparents lived on a postcard perfect cabin on a lake since WWII, or friends who could trace their ancestors back to castles, we decided we were grateful for the opportunity of self-invention.

With age comes confidence. I have no children by choice, like many adoptees. My reason is that with such lousy mom examples, I feared that I could not consistently nurture any child. I have been able to build my tribe of chosen family and I've had the strength to turn away from people who hurt me.

As a newspaper reporter I was fascinated with unfamiliar cultures and countries of origin. While other reporters were more politically correct, I would glom onto a surname and wring out the origins. I was able to enrich so many stories and obituaries by being truly fascinated by family roots and routes through the American experience.

When you're adopted, you only have reprieves from gloomy adoption thoughts. I feel a never-ending push-pull feeling, the imprints of the original and adopted mothers. My first mother wanted the gestating baby to solve all her problems by disappearing.

My second mother wanted the baby me to appear to save her marriage and live out her Life Magazine sugarcoated mother-daughter dreams. When that is your original trauma (being given up) and your great opportunity (a new family) you live with a push and pull soul.

Every impulse has two sides. It is in recognizing this experience and allowing ourselves to make our best choices that we can shake off the dark feeling of being slightly less than whole or not quite deserving.

When new tools come along the 'what-ifs' start percolating again. I recently did an Ancestry.com genetic test to nail down my nationalities of origin. When I got the report, I have to confess, I felt angry. (Liar, liar, pants on fire, birth mother).

After a lifetime of feeling I was Scandinavian and blessing my Viking genes for good heath, I was actually 77 percent British, 12 percent Irish and 12 percent Scandinavian. Which, I know actually means I could still be mostly Scandinavian, because of the cross migration between Britain and Scandinavia. But I missed being "half Finnish" (whatever that means) and I was not happy about sharing Irish origins with my childhood abuser, (although I love Ireland and the Irish people)!

Ancestry.com plays a huge role in my current, and I hope, final identity. A few years ago, I was having a happy period of deep research into my adopted dad's family history. I credit my father, who died in 1996, with being the most positive influence on who I am. It only takes one caring adult to help a child conceived in the dark to thrive in the sunshine.

For example, when I was going through a particularly ugly duckling grade school phase, he told me, "Remember, honey, nobody can resist a joyous woman." Gee, was he ever right.

His final whispered words, chanted repeatedly on his deathbed, "Love is reflected in love," was a deeply imprinted Sunday School message to whoever was listening to always be a loving person. "Love first," he urged many times, "if you want to be loved in this life."

It was only a year or so ago, when a little green leaf popped up on my father's family tree. In a Depression-era census record my father was listed as an "inmate" at Sunny Hills Children's Home in Marin County, California.

Additional research revealed something he kept a secret his whole life: for one year during the darkest time of the Great Depression his parents left their eight-year-old twin sons and older sister at an orphanage. They were unable to feed their children and like many at the time, thought a temporary placement was their only option.

"Your dad cried the whole time," my 91-year-old uncle told me when I asked about it. "I kept telling him, they'd be back. They'll be back, Al," he said. "Your dad had such a horrible time of it."

When you are adopted, there are a million ways to look at your life story. Deep down in every adoptee's psyche is that drumbeat that we were not wanted. It is the monster under the bed, causing doubts and triggering social anxiety.

We can wrestle with it every time we see our bosses talking and think they're going to fire us. We can sell ourselves short by not allowing ourselves to hope that the wonderful guy will propose. We can always, ALWAYS, have an escape route ready because we're not good enough – or, we can decide to let the negative and self-destructive fears go.

I could keep focusing on loss and lies or I could see so many miracles and count my blessings for amazing role models.

The idea that my father, who had been so traumatized as a kid dumped in an orphanage, could adopt not one, but two, lost children and do his very best to inspire them to be capable people, creative and kind, willing and big-hearted, is the place where I was truly born.

I now understand that I existed – at least in my father's heart – way before my conception. The facts of my birth and adoption matter less to me now when I compare them to the inspirational springboard upon which my adopted father launched me into the world. He knew I was special all along and it only took me this long to truly believe it.

Rayne Wolfe

Birth Name: Sally Ann Heiter

Adopted in San Francisco in 1956, Rayne Wolfe was a staff writer (2000 – 2009) at the Santa Rosa Press Democrat (a New York Times regional newspaper). She covered business and philanthropy beats plus everything in between, from penning obituaries to capturing the fun of hometown parades.

With early encouragement from "Mr. San Francisco," columnist Herb Caen, her byline debuted in 1998 with a business column called "What Works" at the San Francisco Sunday Chronicle/Examiner. That column also ran in the Sunday Seattle Times and several other newspapers.

She was a lead blogger at 8WomenDream.com, a site dedicated to encouraging women to work on lifelong dreams. From 2010 to 2012 she was an AOL.com columnist/contributor and helped establish the PetalumaPatch.com bureau. Her freelance work has appeared in the Chicken Soup for the Soul series, Sunset Magazine publications and Glamour Magazine.

In 2014, she published her first book, *Toxic Mom Toolkit*, which includes her memoir describing her three mothers: birth, adoptive and step; as well as the oral histories of other women from around the world who also grew up sane and happy despite having super toxic mothers. Her current focus is on making *Toxic Mom Toolkit* the most popular book (and therapeutic tool) in California prisons.

A former law enforcement chaplain, married to a police Lieutenant, she lives in Petaluma, CA.

Surviving Adoption Aussie Style

by Von Coates

"The question is not how to survive but how to thrive with passion, compassion, humor and style." – Maya Angelou

"It's not what life does to you but what you do to life that counts" – Jim Stymes

It is now seventy years or so since my adoption, which occurred towards the end of a major war and was directly the result of that war. My mother met my father during war training. They came from homes many thousands of miles apart. Both working people, always self-supporting, and somehow making ends meet through hard times.

My father was 32, married with four children, the first of them a girl, who was profoundly shocked to discover when her mother died, that she had been conceived prior to marriage. My own mother was 23, unaware of this wife and family, or so she said, and believed that my father would marry her when he discovered her pregnancy.

She was either very naive, very much in love, deceiving herself, or all three. Perhaps none of those things and it matters little all these years later. I have never judged her. War time meant hard decisions, tough personal challenges, excruciating situations and living on the edge, never knowing what might happen tomorrow. I never asked some of the significant questions – they seemed far too intrusive and personal, even though they relate to my beginning, the critical part of my story. At that time, babies born "out of wedlock," "bastards" or the "illegitimate," whatever you like to call us, were plentiful.

I call my generation of bastards "The Invisible Ones". We were so plentiful, they couldn't give us away! However, we rarely appear in the history of adoption and are conveniently ignored in discussions on adoption because we don't suit the argument.

Adoption timelines never begin early enough to include us and although we and our mothers were so often the victims of forced adoption or at least coercion and expectation, we don't feature. As a Canadian mother-of-loss* informed me, my insistence on inclusion was just a "preoccupation" with a small number of adoptees! In other words, get over it and don't make a fuss about being invisible!

There was no adoption industry in Australia and never has been on the scale of the American adoption industry. Our population was then around 10 million people, but unmarried women and their partners produced enough babies to create a "problem".

The female police officer who set up the first Mother and Baby Home in my State, called us "the unfortunates" – deeming our mothers impoverished, irresponsible refugees from the gutters. She was said to "love the babies as her own" – a tough call for a never married, hard-line Methodist, whose eyes tell a different story.

She looks weary, hard-nosed, full of judgment, a touch cynical even. If she did love us as her own, it was a highly unprofessional stance to take and hopefully she wasn't attempting to show our mothers how it was done, although it wouldn't surprise me!

There were many inhumane practices; we, the babies, were ultimately the victims. We were left to cry in our cots until we cried no more; attention wasn't going to be forthcoming, except at the strictly set feeding times. Our mothers were expected to breast feed us, create a bond, begin to love us and parent us and then to give us up for adoption. It was planned cruelty, a deliberate punishment for the "indiscretions" of our mothers – not our fathers, they got off without even having their names on our birth certificates!

This made it very difficult later for some adoptees, because there was no record anywhere of who our fathers were. If we were lucky enough to meet our mother and she was inclined to tell us, we might learn the name of our father. So many "ifs" and "buts" and so much uncertainty and scope for lies, deliberate misinformation, forgetfulness and the other possibilities of death, dementia, or psychiatric illness.

Personally, I was lucky – my mother had left me a clue by giving me my father's name as my middle name and when we eventually met fifty years after my adoption, she was generous in sharing all the information she knew about him and his ancestry. There is, however, no proof and there will never be proof. Amazingly, I was once asked for proof by a Jigsaw** group, who really should know better, when I was trying to trace a niece lost to adoption!

My father's other offspring just accepted I was who I said I was, even though it caused huge ripples of amazement, disbelief, rejection, acceptance and amusement to run through the family circle. One of my sisters thought my very existence hilarious and treated my appearance as her very own personal "Find My Family."

She visited me out of curiosity and because it made a good story to tell her friends over "drinkies". We had so little in common, but not even a shared father could redeem what was doomed, because she hated him, hated his abuse of our brother, and hated his duplicity.

I met one other sister and was in regular contact with the oldest, who eventually told me she didn't need me to phone her every week now that she was through her cancer scare! I was clearly disposable and I took her at her word. We've never spoken since.

My youngest sister, born five months after me, made it very clear she didn't want anything to do with me. I guess she'd had enough of adoption, after giving her first up for adoption when she was a teen and adopting two boys years later! I was the last straw!

Eventually it became too hard and I gave up on reunion, although was pleased to know my relatives and our history. There was no place for me, arriving as I did out of the blue, at a late stage in all our lives. Had they known about me, a place would have been kept for me at the table and I believe it would have been much easier and had a different outcome.

From The Argus July 18, 1950, in an article entitled "Woman and the Home" there is a quote from Mrs. Mitchell who belonged to The Moral Welfare Association in England. Her views were not uncommon:

"Doctors advocate that illegitimate children should be taken from their mothers at birth and put out to adoption at a fortnight old," Mrs. Mitchell stated, "but the doctors are wrong. The mother should be allowed to have her child with her for at least eight weeks. She must be taught her responsibility for the great disadvantage under which her child was brought into the world. The pain of parting with her child after eight weeks or more may help to keep the unmarried mother straight in her future life."

Others judged this a little harsh, as it didn't take into account the circumstances of the mother. She may have suffered abuse, rape, incest or been unable to make responsible judgments about her situation, due to disability or misinformation.

Adoptees should never be used by adults to push an agenda, publicize adoption, advertise or popularize a cause. So often these days we see adoptees of all ages shamelessly used and exploited in videos, blogs, adoption agency advertisements or in bids for the rights of adults. It seems to be done without malice, but with no forethought, no examination of the consequences and no care about the effects on adoptees currently or in future times. We are being used! Just as we have always been used by adoption to give mothers a way out of a dilemma, adopters a way to make a family and those who support the adoption industry a way to make large amounts of money.

Adoption today is expensive; the cost exorbitant. Back in 1944, there was no cost, because no one had gotten past the problem of unwanted babies or discovered that money could be made from them.

Entrepreneurs in so-called first world countries had only just begun to realize babies were worth money and could be used as leverage, pawns and the means of manipulating power. It was still a time away from so-called second or third world countries discovering that the youngest generation were worth money, could be used influentially and as tourist attractions to bring in revenue. In some countries it has always been known that human beings could be bought and sold for a number of purposes and tragically, we see that trade as strong today, if not stronger, than it has ever been.

I, however, came free, at four weeks old, with no encumbrances, no relatives, no story, no history, no promises, no expectations and was as truly as much a " blank slate" as they could make me.

As is often the case, people like to attach information to adoptees, very often wrong information, outright lies and untruths, sometimes deliberately, sometimes out of "kindness," "concern" or because somewhere there is a jolt of conscience about what is being done.

In my case, my adoptive father says he was given some information about my mother by a person he couldn't remember. He was deliberately vague. It was a major red herring and kept my mother from me for an additional decade. During that time, the law changed and Australian adoptees were able to receive their original birth certificates and birth information.

In addition, in my State, a register was kept so that those mothers or biological relatives and adoptees wishing to meet could have that facilitated by experienced workers. My mother and I both registered in the same month and were in contact shortly afterwards, having been treated as responsible adults, with courtesy and rapidity.

Looking back, I have no complaints and our reunion went smoothly. I had spent many years involved in reunion work and in preparing for my own reunion. None of that preparation time is ever wasted; it is helpful, necessary and well spent. I would recommend as much reading on the subject as possible and facing the challenges with therapy or counseling, in order to deal with the effects of adoption. I am a firm believer in the many stages of the adopted life and that each stage has its own unique challenges to be faced.

This is how we survive adoption and if we work at it, we thrive, live good lives in which we contribute, learn and are successful in what we do. To overcome the major tasks is a significant achievement. Some things may always elude us. We can heal, but there may be scars. There may be significant damage to our health brought about by stress in utero or other conditions not conducive to our development.

When you look at the effects of our mother-loss and of adoption, and detail some of the results, it is scarcely surprising it can take a life time to deal with – we may suffer feelings of rejection, abandonment, guilt, grief and loss or complex loss with attendant anger, numbness, depression, anxiety, fear.

We may find self-discovery difficult; for me the learning is always slow and the insights take time. I take a long time to process what I call "relationship information" and it took me years, decades even, to realize that identity is a fluid, ever-changing part of us, which does not remain fixed. We can be whoever we want to be!

The full force of community and religious disapproval descended on our mothers and on us as innocent babies. Fortunately it was not so with all those who were found to adopt us. My own adoptive parents were not so judgmental and while I was considered a 'blank slate', as was the way of the times, they never gave me information about my mother which was critical or disapproving.

They didn't have it to give and the red herring my adoptive father produced when I was thirty-two is a whole other story, as our own story as a family had moved on to a point where he preferred to disown me!

The problem of the times lay in what to do with us bastards. Eventually advertisements appeared asking for adoptive parents, kind people who could raise us, save us from orphanage life and give us a family life in which we were cared for, hopefully loved where all stigma would be removed, because no one knew our stories. A quick survey of the printed material of the times shows a general concern for the welfare of children being adopted and an awareness of the possibilities of lack of care, if assessment was not done and if there was no monitoring.

They must have been hopeful times, when it was believed we could be 'blank slates', that no harm would come from adoption and that stigma would not attach itself to us if our histories were unknown. Those of us who live the adopted life know only too well that there is no 'blank slate'; all of us have a history which can never be wiped out, however people may try to achieve that and the stigma never disappears.

Even those adoptees who were not told of their adoptions and discovered by various means at various ages tell us that they have often felt disquiet about their family connections, their place in a family and about the information they had or had not been given. The means of discovery are many and varied, usually shocking and mostly painful, producing a sense of betrayal, disillusion, anger and mistrust amongst others.

How many of my fellow adoptees have been told, "I wish we had never adopted you" or "You were never one of us" and so on. Mothers tell us they wish they'd had an abortion and any number of cruel and crude expressions of their hatred for how we changed their lives, how they don't want to know us or ever hear about us again. Others of course, tell us they loved and wanted us and were forced to abandon us, sometimes by those with influence and power – church elders, religious leaders, disapproving communities, matriarchs and patriarchs, employers, defense forces personnel and so on.

Others keep us dangling like puppets, playing us along, waxing hot and cold, wanting us to keep their secrets, wanting us to remain their "dirty little secret," the skeleton in the closet. When an adoptee brings such a relationship to a close, it is often a time of celebration, because it means they have found the strength and determination to run their own ship, be their own person and refuse to play games of domination, to be bullied, diminished and accorded second place.

We so often see mothers play these games on a wider stage with adoptees they don't know and they tell them they are "wallowing in misery," ridicule and treat them with disrespect and a serious disregard for the truth of adoption for adoptees.

The myths they hold dear about adoptees are no longer sustainable, because adoptees have found their voices. They have formed a world-wide community where they compare notes, exchange views and are active together for change.

Adult adoptees are sometimes accused by adopters and prospective adopters of trying to spoil "the beauty of adoption" by telling the truth about adoption, by bringing reality into a world where souls are saved, orphans rescued, families made – and adults made parents.

There will always be children who benefit from not being raised in an orphanage, children who could be reunited with family if poverty did not prevail, children who are disabled who could benefit from better treatment, conditions and care, adults who should never be parents, children who would have a better life if they weren't tourist attractions, children who should never be adoptees, and mothers who should never be separated from their children.

In a better, more humane, less greedy world, where the needs of the vulnerable come first, we could do much, much better. We could begin by making sure all adoptees are not second-class citizens, have their rights and have access to their birth information, their records and their relatives. We could make sure all children remain with their biological relatives in their own community and that they have the means to thrive. We could ensure the safety of all children and find families only for those who need them because they have come from dysfunctional, abusive homes.

We could ensure that all adults have access to reliable, free contraception which is easy to use and accepted by their community because education has been adequate. We could educate for responsible, informed parenting, because being a parent is the most important task there is. Perhaps all of those are nothing compared with the enormity of ensuring governments act ethically, take a new and humane view of adoption and make it a priority to ensure no child lives without food, fresh water, clothes, security and a safe loving household.

Here in Australia some of us are very concerned about our current government's approach to adoption. The aim is to simplify it, speed up the processes and make more adoptees "available." This may mean adopting children who are trafficked and from countries which are not signatories to the Hague Convention. Domestic adoption rates have fallen dramatically.

In my State they are nil, because mothers are keeping their babies and have no intention of considering adoption. There is no enormously profitable, thriving adoption industry, although fundamentalist Christian groups are promoting adoption, encouraging adoption and are enthusiastic supporters of orphan adoption, using figures which do not show the realistic numbers of children who are actually real orphans.

To save a soul is considered sufficient grounds for adoption and this has not to date been a prevalent view in my country. Currently we have children born in detention, some of these children are stateless, without nationality. It is yet to be decided if they will be given Australian nationality. As an adult adoptee, my question is whether their parents will also be given nationality or asylum and what that will mean for the children. I hope we will not be seeing an increase in adoptions as punishment for those who seek asylum. With our current government anything seems possible!

In recent years we witnessed an Apology by the Federal Government to The Stolen Generation and an Apology to the victims of forced adoption. This was the first time anywhere in the world that adoptees had been recognised as being victims of adoption, of suffering trauma and loss because of it and it was a significant milestone for adoption activists who had worked hard on various aspects of the Apology.

It was an achievement for all adoptees everywhere. My own State was one of the first to apologise and I witnessed it first hand, with my family, in the House – a moving and important day for me and for all those who accepted the Apology and found it useful. I was told by a father-of-loss that I needed psychiatric help for having accepted the Apology, presumably because he is one of a small band of people who believe compensation is more important than recognition, apology, and being able to move forward.

Many of our fellow adoptees in other parts of the world would welcome the day when they are lucky enough to be in the position we adult Australian adoptees are today.

Many people, from all sides of adoption, worked hard, continuously and judiciously, to get us here. For those parents-of-loss who complain that adoptees rode on their backs – if that is true, they surely owe us, it is the least they could do for us.

All of us who were victims of forced adoption from whatever time and place, deserve apology, consideration, and hopefully new understanding. We hope to see the day when it is universal, when all adoptees have all their information and rights and when adoption is rare. Until that time, we will continue to share our stories, insist on change and work towards our future.

*Parents-of-loss are mothers and fathers who have lost children to adoption. In Australia, some of them were active in pushing our Federal Government for an Inquiry into forced adoption. When that was achieved through hard work, persistence and endurance, adoptees began to see it was appropriate that they should make Submissions to the Inquiry since many had been victims of forced adoption. This was unpopular amongst some parents-of-loss who tried to suggest adoptees were not qualified or that we were riding on the backs of those who had achieved the Inquiry.

**An Australian organisation that provides information, counselling, search and intermediary services to people separated from family for many different reasons.

Von Coates

Born in 1944, Von's parents met in the RAAF and produced a "love child," for which adoption was the only option. Von was raised in a small Australian country community. At 21, she went to live in London, returning home to live almost 30 years later. She was reunited with her mother after 50 years, met some of her father's other offspring and knows a lot of family history. A firm foundation for the adopted life, giving birth to a daughter and being present at the South Australian Apology for forced adoption are some of the highlights so far.

Lost in Others' Translation...Loving Your True Self

by Stephani Harris

I can recall looking into mirrors noticing how my eyes would pass me this blank stare. It was a look that led me away, feeling fearful for the day ahead. It was a fear of not recognizing what kind of day was before me, the possibility of receiving bad news, or any messages of surprise. I would never share my sadness and disconnection to others. Instead, I sought to make others laugh and feel something other than what I felt.

What I later found was the urgent need to know the truth about my adoption as a newborn. Confusion came into my path before the truth. My adoption was revealed at nine-years-old. I was young enough to be confused but old enough to understand that adoption was different and an event that would forever change my life.

I was adopted as a newborn with adoptive parents and maternal biological family from the same small town in Kentucky. In the era of my adoption, my adopted family never had any pre-adoption classes. This was a case of two families in a small town who were only acquaintances. One family desiring another child and the natural mother only wanting to do what she felt was in the best interest for her and the unborn child. No large amount of legal paperwork, an attorney, fifty dollars and a pen to make it legal. That simple, right?

At times, it was awkward and confusing. We were all friendly strangers that smiled and waved to one another at a respectful distance, as though no changing hands of a newborn baby occurred. It wasn't until my preteens that I realized my cousins were more than just my play friends. They were my natural family. I did feel betrayed to some degree by the ones who knew the secret. This adoption story must have been a bad thing if it was a secret, right? Most secrets result from misgivings, shame and guilt.

Throughout my childhood and adult life people close to me would say that I was hypersensitive and if we discussed the adoption topic, then it would create more pain for myself and everyone else involved.

When I did speak up about my feelings and had questions, it was difficult for my adoptive parents to understand me. As I spoke, I felt as though I was inside a sound proof bubble, asking questions but no sound was coming outside the bubble to be heard.

The "child in me" remained silent and the more I remained silent, the "teen in me" became filled with silent anger and pain. As I became older, I avoided allowing family and friends to get to know me on a deeper level. I successfully avoided others leaning or hanging out on the wall that I built up from my false sense of identity and sadness. The "who am I really" confusion in the mirror stemmed from the false messages of "being a mistake" or feeling that "I should have never been born."

My birth mother's decision to relinquish me to another family was sincerely for my best interest. I fully understand that it was not an easy decision and I do give her the utmost respect. I've made my choice to not judge her (or anyone involved) for what she felt was the best for all involved. Regardless of all the reasons surrounding my natural mother's decision to relinquish me, I strongly feel I was placed where I was destined to be.

There is no right or wrong way in how I have experienced my adoption journey nor do I expect others to accept my views. I have accepted the fact that we all have a history full of mistakes. Many mistakes led to secrets but it's 'us' that end up putting the shame and guilt on our mistakes. Society and others around us can place shame and guilt on us for what we have done, but ultimately it's up to us to stop the vicious cycle.

I was at a point in my life where I needed to know the full truth about who was staring back at me in the mirror so I began to start searching for my birth father. I became even more curious when I discovered that the primary reason for my relinquishment was because my birth father was a different race than my birth mother.

I've had most of my questions answered, but along with those rewards, have been many ups, downs, rejections and embraces. I am grateful for the ample amount of acceptance, love and mutual respect from both biological families. It's still an ongoing journey of healing and acceptance of me with both of my biological and adopted families. Of course, it hasn't been easy, but everything that I've felt worth fighting for, has naturally purged me out of my comfort zones.

My husband is also an adoptee. He was placed in foster care at birth and was adopted by his foster family soon thereafter. He had a closed adoption and for much of his adult life, never had an interest in seeking out his biological family. It wasn't until he had some medical questions, that he then began to have a sincere desire to seek out his biological family. In a two-year, nail-biting wait for the Judge to order his adoption records to be opened, he finally was able to begin his identity journey. Last year, he met his birth mother and half siblings for the first time.

He continues to have contact with his birth mother and siblings. In the honeymoon stage/first time meetings, as with most reunions, the excitement and findings are full of joy, fears, and jealousy. As he continues to go through the stages of reunion and discovery, we have become one another's support system. We share a common denominator with our understanding of the experience with both closed and open adoptions. It's been challenging, yet rewarding to be married to someone with similar triggers and issues. He has been the perfect husband, my cheerleader, a safe protector, and my best friend.

To this day when most of our family, friends, and acquaintances share their great wisdom (to make us feel better when we discuss or have been asked about our adoption journey) we commonly are told, "Oh honey, you should be grateful to be alive, someone cared enough to adopt you and take you in as their own," or "Sweetheart, you should 'just' be thankful that you were not aborted!" Of course, that all may be true for those who are not adopted and looking from the outside in, but, in reality, minimizing our adoption experience only maximizes our pain.

Personally, these types of statements have never brought me serenity and healing, but have silenced me more to not feel or gain trust in sharing my feelings. For those who may have said similar statements to adoptees or family members whose birth mother or father were not in their lives, I am not throwing shame or guilt your way. I am simply asking for you to listen more and speak less.

I would rather be a tick on a dog's testicle than hear those words from someone telling me or others how we should or should not feel. I, nor any other adoptee that I know, has ever felt a peace that surpasses all understanding that someone "wanted me" or that "I wasn't aborted".

The words may give comfort to someone in a survivor or denial mode, but it doesn't answer all the questions that we deserve, nor does it help, edify, or lift us up in our quest for the truth.

I still struggle at certain times with people pleasing, caretaking others, and concerns about when, why and how others view me. It's a long and slow process and I'm learning to not put my focus on the opinion and advice of others who are not safe. It started in finding a great support system – my amazing therapist who is familiar with trauma and loss. After working with her, my fear is diminished when small or big changes happen suddenly or when I am concerned about what the next hour may bring, or when my fears of failing to give the correct answer of "yes or no" from the ones who've expected more from me, surface.

After all, many adoptees are people pleasers and we find ourselves easily pulled into this pit of wanting acceptance from others so we don't disappoint them. I used to twist, position, hold and then wait to see if others approved of the way I felt or reacted. It's as though many of us find ourselves functioning as an "emotional chameleon". I have come to the realization that I no longer need others' acceptance as I become stronger in knowing the truth surrounding my birth identity and healing from the false messages that I took on as a child and an adult.

If you are an adoptee, soon to be an adoptive parent, or you may be a birth parent that relinquished your child, we all have so many questions. Many questions run through our minds. Our questions have been:

How crucial is it for us, as adoptees, to know the truth and is the truth more important for some than for others?

Once we find out the truth about our story, will it create more of a peace of mind or will the truth lead us into more rejection?

In seeking out answers to our questions, will others be hurt, and will this lead our potential family members and their families into turmoil?

How much of the truth do we deserve to know?

Will we intrude on our new families' lives? Do we have the right to do so?

Did I get my mannerisms from learned behavior or genetics? Do I share the way I walk and carry myself with someone else? How about the shape of my nose, eyes, mouth, wide hips, big butt and the wrinkle between my eyes?

I have found that most people who are already familiar with their own family background and ancestry are usually the ones who have a harder time in understanding the urgency for us to know about ours. My heart is always heavy with compassion for thousands of other fellow adoptees who haven't found the answers with door after door being shut in their faces.

Today, living in truth and acceptance of me, I am blessed beyond measure regardless of my circumstances. I feel no one is to blame as to the whys, hows or when I was conceived and adopted. It's our journey and no one else needs any blame, shame or guilt thrown their way. I tried that for a short period of time and it only continued to prevent me from finding out my need to know the person staring back at me in the mirror. I was lost in translation. But now I have found her. I found her face through her own acceptance and love. Her name is Stephani.

Adoptee Survival Tips:

1. Be easy on yourself. Learn to know you have permission to feel and react.

2. When you are rejected by any of your adopted and natural families, remember that it is not you that they are rejecting (they may have been rejecting others in their lives before you even came into the picture).

3. Find safe people to talk to. Not everyone is interested in your journey and understands your loss.

4. It's okay for others to not understand you. Your healing is not dependent on anyone else's understanding.

5. When finding your truth and identity, remember everyone will not be happy and delighted (they were not always happy or delighted before you came into the picture).

6. Expect the unexpected in your reunions. Adoption truth is about our birthright (the truth can bring out the best and the worst in others).

7. Be true to yourself and know there is a true freedom in being your authentic self.

8. If possible, don't rush into a quick decision. Sleep on it for a day and then take the next step to make that call or write that letter. If you fail, remember it's okay to fail. You are not being graded on this test.

9. If doors have been shut in reaching out to your birth parents, write a letter to them, expressing your hurt. Go ahead and write out the questions, your anger, etc. Keep the letters in your safe spot. Our main objective is to heal without the need to find approval.

Stephani Harris lives in Louisville, Kentucky with her loving husband, who is also an adoptee from a closed adoption and her 150 lb. Big Bear Akita (also adopted). She also has an adopted stepdaughter who currently lives in St. Louis.

She is a business owner of over 20 years, a Salon Master Educator, and serves as a professional mentor in the salon business industry encouraging professional development. She has studied Internal Family Systems Therapy by Richard Schwartz for her personal growth and has been actively involved with IFS group therapy for over five years focusing on healing of grief, loss, and trauma/PTSD.

www.Facebook.com/stephani.harris
www.Selfleadership.org

After Delusions, Breakdowns, and Misdiagnoses – Recovery and Healing

by Laura Dennis

The EMTs asked a series of questions, which I answered like the crazy person I'd become, including my suspicions that I was either drugged or impregnated or very sick or worse. Even so, I was aware enough of my surroundings to avoid specifically mentioning the Illuminati, just in case one of the EMTs was a spy.

I was transported to the local hospital and tested. The results came back: no drugs in my system, no trauma to my body, and no, I wasn't pregnant. The nurse said I needed to be taken to a different hospital. During my intake interview at the somewhat scary public mental hospital, I truly believed the nurse I was talking to was my childhood friend, Tess. I was surprised that she had become a nurse and was no longer a schoolteacher in Georgia, but nevertheless I was comforted to have her there with me.

At this point, I lost track of chunks of time. It felt like I stayed one night in the public mental hospital. I remember darkness when I spoke to my adoptive mom and told her that she was also a spy. It was still dark when I pretended to take the pills that the nurse handed me. The mania had transformed into what psychology might call a "mixed state," not exactly mania, but mania mixed with depressive thoughts.

For example, I didn't feel suicidal in a depressed sort-of-way, but my sorrow over 9/11 transformed into a guilt so deep I was soon willing to hurt myself and put my life at risk just to escape it. I stayed long enough to mingle in the common area with the other patients. One man said he was Jesus. Naturally, I believed him one hundred percent. I mean, he had the religious tattoos to prove it. I sympathized and considered the possibility that I was Mary Magdalene, the supposed Biblical whore and perhaps Jesus' lover. I disregarded the notion quickly, as this particular Jesus simply didn't seem to be my type.

My delusions continued. It's not lost on me that my ideations were based in Judeo-Christian mythology. The mind, even when confused, goes with what it knows, and my religious brainwashing ran deep. With little sleep, nothing to eat – hospital food was nasty – and no drugs to calm me down, my mind completely stepped into an alternate reality. I deduced the only plausible explanation for all of this was that clearly, I was a robot. Not a doot-doot-doot, move-stiffly-and-do-fast-mathematical-calculations robot.
.

No, I was a bionic woman type of robot.

I had been born this way. To cover up my true nature, I'd been adopted, given a "real" birth certificate as a member of the Dennis family. My dance training had provided a physical basis for my excellent fighting skills. Whoever had created me also had ultimate control over my brain. I'd been given to an adoptive father who was also a member of the Masonic Temple, in order to protect me and to keep my true origins a secret.

But during my childhood, a nefarious organization had clandestinely taken power from the Masons and assumed control of my mental wiring as well. So when it was time to find someone to carry out 9/11, my "handlers" had turned to me, activating my programming. I had been reprogrammed and then triggered to act without my knowledge, unwittingly becoming a terrorist capable of flying a plane directly into the World Trade Center.

If this all sounds very elaborate and implausible, that's because you're not delusional. Congratulations. However, in my manic state, my thoughts went on overdrive. The basic explanation came down to this subconscious knowledge: I was guilty for the undoing of my adoptive family. All of the delusions were simply colorful party favors that explained away my deep-seeded shame at abandoning my family.

When I finally entered therapy, my first two questions were:

Am I crazy?

Specifically, am I bipolar?

Perhaps my psychiatrist didn't want to say I was bipolar and make my ongoing prognosis a self-fulfilling prophesy. Maybe she really didn't know. She talked a lot about the stress of "life changes." Apparently, when you're going through one or two, even if they're good news – you got a great new job in a new city, for example – you should try to limit other life changes.

So for me, since I was (1) starting grad school (2) in a new city, I should have avoided other stressors, which in 2001 included: (3) reuniting with my first mother and her extended family, (4) planning a wedding, (5) calling off said wedding, ultimately breaking up with fiancé, (6) quitting my job, (7) adoptive parents separating, (8) father consequently suicidal and hospitalized, (9) death in the family. And, number (10) national crisis (9/11). Is that even included as a possibility?

If the fact that I had been adopted at birth and was suffering from unaddressed post-adoption issues was deemed important, no one mentioned it. Truly, the whole reunion itself was enough of a life event to warrant not doing anything else in the meantime. However, at the time, no one discussed the emotional loss and grief of adoption as a possible root cause of my emotional turmoil. That's not to say being adopted caused me to be bipolar, or better said, to have a mental breakdown that was very similar to a bipolar breakdown. It's simply that unaddressed post-adoption issues can lead to problems with self-identity, attachment, relationships, and attendant feelings of guilt, shame and worthlessness.

Nevertheless, this psychiatrist emphasized that if I had another breakdown and had to be hospitalized, well yes, I was bipolar. I might or might not have a chemical imbalance in my brain, the cause of which might or might not be hereditary. (Although, she never did ask me about family history of mental illness.) And if I did get myself manic again, my breakdown would likely be worse than this one. But if I could control my waves of depression and mania, we could chalk this breakdown up as just a one-of caused by too many life changes in too short a time.

I was skeptical, but she had handed me a challenge. No more psychotic episodes. Got it.

So what has all of this got to do with self-help?

The delusions, the breakdown, the hospital stay … the medications, the therapy, the going-off-the-meds-cold-turkey … the so-called recovery … all of that was not enough.

It wasn't enough to lose my mind. It wasn't enough to survive. It wasn't enough to try with all of my being each and every day to avoid becoming manic; to avoid sliding into a depressive episode.

You may be wondering: What more was there to do? You didn't kill yourself! You recovered!

Yes and no.

The six months of heavy-duty meds, the two years of therapy, the guilt and shame over what I had done to myself, the daily monitoring of my moods … all of that was a Band-Aid.

In cognitive behavioral therapy with a psychologist, we addressed ways to move forward, how to watch my mood and my daily actions. My therapist did a wonderful job bringing my awareness to the über-negative inner train-of-thoughts that ruled my day. (You're fat, you should work out more, you should eat less, you're a shitty dancer, you'll never measure up, you'll never find someone, and on and on.)

However, whenever I brought up my delusions, or tried to analyze what was going on with them, the psychologist doggedly changed the course of the discussion. In his defense, he probably thought that he was keeping me from becoming manic, but the reality was that I needed to make sense of the delusions in order to process and heal.

Writing helped. But it wasn't necessarily the initial journaling that did it. Later on, when I started writing my memoir, it was the actual process of putting together a coherent story for others to read and understand that helped me make great leaps forward. Aside from sorting out the delusions and describing them in a linear fashion, I had to ask myself things like:

Why, in my manic state, did I believe I was the cause of my adopted uncle's death in the Twin Towers?

What was it about becoming a bionic robot that made my mind believe I could solve everything?

The reality I needed to come to terms with was that believing that I caused a national tragedy was my overwrought mind's way of dealing with the guilt I felt over reuniting with my first mother and leaving my hometown. (Remember, delusions are extreme and symbolic, and of course, open to interpretation. This is the conclusion I've come to.) In essence, I felt responsible for the happiness of my adoptive parents, and I thought that I'd failed since they were getting a divorce.

The bionic robot ideation was an extreme manifestation of the "perfect adoptee" I'd tried to be my entire life. If I could just be good enough, get perfect grades, not cause trouble … I'd be worthy of not being given away again. I'd show that I was "good enough" to reunite with my first mother, that the pain of my separation from her was worth it because I'd accomplished so many material goals.

It was only by thinking and writing through to these conclusions that I realized the guilt and the perfectionism were unhealthy. I had to let go of these – and so many other, long-held notions of what it meant to be a good person, a good adoptee. But there was something else that was necessary in my healing process, and it blows my mind that no one ever thought to offer this to me earlier.

Finally, FINALLY, as a result of starting my blog, Expat Adoptee Mommy, I reached out and connected with the online adoptee community, opening my eyes to the commonalities that we share. Of course, I haven't met another adoptee who believed they were a bionic spy who inadvertently caused 9/11. Even I know that's absurd!

What I mean is, this sense of guilt, this ambition to be perfect, this undeniable drive to search and reunite, this need to find meaning in my life – were all emotions and desires common to the adoptee experience. To come to terms with my adoption, ultimately to be able to put the delusions in context and let go of the pain; I had to reach out to others who had been there, who were still there, living this adopted life.

So in the end, the recovery was, and is, ongoing. Honestly, I still go back and re-process that time period in my life, weaving in the things I learn from others in the adoption community. The medications and the therapy helped, but only to a certain extent. The self-help and true recovery came through processing my own personal experience in my own time, and connecting that experience with others who had lived it too. The process is ongoing, but at least I now have the tools and the relationships I need.

Excerpted and adapted from Adopted Reality, A Memoir. Find the entire spy delusion and recovery story on Amazon.

Laura Dennis was born and adopted in New Jersey and raised in Maryland. She earned a B.A. and M.F.A. in dance performance and choreography, but gave up aches and pains and bloody feet in 2004 to become a stylish sales director for a biotech startup.

Then with two children under the age of three, in 2010 she and her husband sought to simplify their lifestyle and escaped to his hometown, Belgrade. While the children learned Serbian in their cozy preschool, Laura recovered from sleep deprivation and wrote *Adopted Reality, A Memoir*, available on Amazon.

An adoptee activist in reunion, she writes at The Lost Daughters, Adoption Voices Magazine and her own blog, Expat (Adoptee) Mommy. Her essays have been published in *Lost Daughters: Writing Adoption from a Place of Empowerment and Peace*, *The Perpetual Child, Dismantling the Stereotype, Adult Adoptee Anthology*, and *Dear Wonderful You, Letters to Adopted & Fostered Youth*.

She is passionate about giving voice to the adoptee experience and is proud to have edited the popular anthologies, *Adoption Reunion in the Social Media Age* (Entourage Publishing) and *Adoption Therapy: Perspectives from Clients and Clinicians on Processing and Healing Post-Adoption Issues* (Entourage Publishing).

Adoptees and Boundaries

by Karen Brown Belanger

Our roles within our families define us. From birth, we begin to discover ourselves within these roles, our genetics, and our family histories. The boundaries we learn growing up create a definite measure of who we are and who we become. Adoptees often struggle with boundaries because our origins are many-times unknown, our places within families are different, and the people around us may not understand that our world may feel different, than it does for the non-adopted.

It seems for many of us, there are no real and recognizable boundaries for where we begin and end. The security non-adopted persons derive from known facts about who they are and where they come from are invisible, for the most part, and unrecognized by them. To adoptees, it is as blatant and evident as the noses on our faces – the noses and faces we may have no idea from where they originate. Non-adopted persons can literally reach out and grasp proof of who they are within a family.

A family created by adoption has different dynamics it brings to the family table. Adoptees' roles and designated lines are blurred. And, we may have no vocabulary to describe how this makes us feel. Without these tangible lines drawn in our lives, our boundaries may become weak or nonexistent and can easily change with every moment and situation that occurs in our lives.

Many of us have had the most basic human rights taken from us: the right to be with our family of origin and the right to access most information about them. We've been placed where we've had no say or right to be anything less than grateful for the unrecognized loss we have endured. Then, expectations are heaped upon us to fill the lives of others with love and joy. It's no real surprise then that many adoptees have huge issues and problems with boundaries.

I grew up and learned to become chameleon-like. I didn't even realize this until I was older. I assumed the personalities and behavior my adoptive family expected in addition to whatever peer group or organization I belonged to, or was trying to belong to. I knew I didn't belong within my adoptive family as we were and are polar opposites. Lacking in knowledge of my genetic and hereditary origins, I didn't trust what I felt, who I was, where I was going, or where I belonged. I was boundary-less.

I was easily convinced to try or do anything and was willing to compromise my own personal values just to be accepted. I could not say no to anyone or anything. There were times I broke out of that mold and spoke from my true character but at the first sign of reprimand or disapproval, I quickly withdrew back into my shell.

I became a people pleaser and a door mat. Better to acquiesce to what others want and need than to be rejected. And it always came back to the fact that as an adoptee, I was rejected by the two people (or more in my case) that should have been the most important people to me on the planet. Sometimes as adoptees we pretend and become what others want in order to gain acceptance because we do not have the ability to give it to ourselves.

Unfortunately I became semi-promiscuous at a young age. I say semi because I really don't want to face the fact that in my late teens and early twenties I would have had sex with almost any guy who would pay attention to me. If I said no, then I believed he wouldn't like me. It took me a very long time to discover that guys trying to get sex didn't like me whether I gave in or not.

Neither did most of the other people I was pleasing to be accepted. It took me a long time in relationships to incorporate healthy sexual boundaries. The lack of boundaries spilled over into every area of my life and became quite confusing, frustrating, and depressing.

After therapy and codependency work and the realization of my lack of healthy boundaries, I began to implement strategies to improve my work and personal relationships. I admit this was not easy, far from it, in fact. Drastic change is extremely difficult especially when it is rooted so deeply in who we are and have been since we can remember.

One of the first realizations I came to was I was always the person everyone turned to in need. If there was a birthday party, wedding, shower, or funeral, Karen was the one to call to bring food, organize and help throw the party, and faithfully, without waiver, show up no matter what was going on in my own life. I set this all in motion when I began volunteering in the beginning so I could become important to someone. I received validation when my skills and talents, along with reliability, proved I was worthy of the tasks and responsibilities given to me. Therefore, I was a worthy person.

It took a few years before I was healthy enough to realize that when it came to my own life events, especially birthdays, no one was available. Phone calls were not quickly returned, promises of outings and gatherings were forgotten or canceled, and nothing was reciprocal in any capacity.

When I stopped picking up the phone to call, all communication quickly and abruptly ended. Until, of course, the next crisis or emergency or request of me for A-Z. I had always been able to do the whole gamut of support for everyone, almost anytime, on short notice. I also knew if I didn't show up or didn't adhere to the exact details I was given, for whatever it was I had been asked to do, I would be reprimanded in some passive aggressive manner.

I knew I had to clean relationship house without making it a big deal. Why? Because I became strong enough to finally voice my hurt and pain in a calm and adult manner over the inequality in these relationships that was obvious to me but not to them at all. Yet nothing ever changed. These relationships were extremely important to me and had been for twenty years. However, they were not healthy relationships because I had not been healthy enough then to create decent boundaries that would dictate any equality of treatment.

I first had to admit that I had played a large part in the imbalance in my relationships. I had and was allowing others to override my own gut instinct and desires. I had to bear witness to and attest to the facts that I was not a helpless victim in all of it, and that only I could change this way of thinking and behaving.

We are powerless to change negative situations if we can't face self-examination. Some adoptees may not have good boundaries but many do have inner walls created when very young to protect from further loss. We need to tear down walls that we have built as defense mechanisms so we can allow ourselves to acknowledge the primal pain and wounds and the havoc they may have wreaked upon us, so we can vanquish their destructive effects, and create a healthy intimacy with ourselves and with other people.

We need to return to who we were before we began the dependency, pretending, and denying. We need to find ourselves first before we can put healthy boundaries into a strong reliable position.

While we may not be able to do this early in our lives, because we may not have had a true understanding or comprehension of our circumstances, we can embrace who and what we really are now.

The setting of healthy boundaries allows us to grow and develop in ways we could not before. In order to reclaim ourselves, we must risk rejection again while standing firm in support of what is best for us in the long run. When we actualize our authentic selves, we may become temporarily uncomfortable with others, but in the end, we gain self-respect and empowerment.

So how do we break patterns we may have developed so young from situations that could not be handled with truth and honesty? How can we change our actions and reactions so we can become unstuck in perpetual detrimental behaviors? What fears are the basis of our actions, reactions, and interactions with others?

Give up the illusion someone else will make you happy. I've found that a common trait with some adoptees is we may try to find ourselves in others. We can become easily lost and absorbed by others if we do not have healthy boundaries. This may stem from issues of control and may sometimes lead to us becoming easy targets for bullies. And, adoptees are not the only ones with trauma and issues playing out in their lives. People are human and full of their own dysfunction and agendas.

Don't keep company with those who constantly push your boundaries and require you to expend unnecessary energy saying no or make you feel bad because you won't or worse, that you can't do what they ask. This can be especially tough to do at work with superiors. Some people are used to getting their way and they can make your life miserable, if you allow it. Some people won't hear your "no" or believe it unless you become harsh with them and then it becomes your issue instead.

When you are centered and anchored in who you really are, you will have healthy boundaries set in place. Not barricades of exclusion or flimsy and easily surmounted walls, but firm and established boundaries that function well. Now when I say no, I mean no. Not a wishy-washy half apology with a side of guilt afterward. I am also learning to say no without explaining to everyone why. Most people don't care why you can or can't do something anyway. They are more focused on the result and outcome rather than the reason.

Consistency is paramount and practice is pertinent. You can't say no and then waffle when the guilt begins to override your own common sense. I often times find myself wanting to pick the phone back up or message back advising that I'm available instead of standing strong in my original answer. But the difference is now; I don't act on that, because I know the importance of balance and boundaries in my life.

I have fewer friends now but I no longer need the approval of others or let my boundaries down for a temporary fix of approval and self-worth. I still struggle with work boundaries though I am finding self-approval much easier. Perhaps that comes with age and experience but such is life for non-adopted persons as well.

However, many adoptees are set up from the beginning to go down the path of least resistance and unhealthy boundary placements.

I can say searching and finding facts and information about my biological family has given me a renewed sense of hope about discovering who I really am genetically. Along with that knowledge comes a stronger purpose in evolving into as complete a person as I possibly can. Included within that evolving are distinctly constructed healthy boundaries.

At the end of the day, most people just want to be happy. But, happiness usually also comes in living with healthy intact boundaries. It governs all of our relationships in life. This might be challenging and certainly startling to others when your role in their lives change, as you change your life. But those close to you might notice a different more positive person, one who is not living with the shame, anger, or guilt directed at them or others over an inability to say no, or to ask for what you really need and want.

There are now fewer complaints and fewer judgments from others because I have redirected myself and my life in a confident and assertive manner. I know I am enjoying the respect I feel from others now as well as from myself when I am focused on making choices with clear and decisive intent.

I'm glad to see so many adoptees now speaking up about their own personal battles with the issues adoption has brought to their lives and individual experiences. It has made all the difference for so many adoptees and brought a great deal of education to the public who had little knowledge, if any, about the realities of adoption.

Adoption has come a long way in the last two decades from the archaic and outdated system it once functioned as, and from out of the secrets it has functioned in. I am thankful that many adoptees have found the courage and strength to risk criticism, judgment, and ridicule, and transformed not only their own lives, but the lives of other adoptees as well.

Karen Brown Belanger is an adult adoptee and the author of *Assembling Self,* an adoption poetry book, and writes at her blog of the same name. She contributes at The Lost Daughters bloggers and was recently included in the *Lost Daughters: Writing Adoption from a Place of Empowerment and Peace*.

Karen has held various leadership positions within the adoption education, reform, and activism community over the last fifteen years. She recently submitted a piece included in *Adoption Therapy: Perspectives from Clients and Clinicians on Processing and Healing Post-Adoption Issues* (Entourage Publishing) and is now working on her second book.

She inherited her biological mother's love of dance, cooking from scratch, growing roses, and her biological great grandmother's musical talent. Karen is married and the mother of three adult children. In her spare time she also enjoys reading, working out, and helping other adoptees on their paths towards healing.

Finding Peace Being Adopted

by Marla Jones

I sat at the art table in my kindergarten class listening to a boy talk about how he was adopted.

"What does adoption mean?" I asked.

He said something to the extent of, "That's when your first parents can't raise you and they give you to someone else who can raise you."

"Will you ever see your first parents again?"

"No, I don't think so."

"How sad. Don't you miss your first parents? I think I would want to go back and visit them."

Then another girl looked across the table directly at me and said, "What do you mean? You're adopted too, stupid."

Being the wise age of five and not wanting to look any more stupid than I already did, "Oh," was all I could muster up to say.

So I accepted the fact that I was adopted, just like that, yet I was never at peace with it growing up.

I was fortunate to grow up amongst many other friends who were adopted so I never felt different from other kids in the sense of having the term "adopted" tagged to my identity. But inside I felt that I just didn't belong in the life that I was living.

I couldn't put words to it (until much later) but I knew something wasn't right. I was always trying to guess at who I was really meant to be. Yet there was no starting point in which to begin a journey to find out. There was no information offered and none to be found so I felt trapped.

On top of the issues I faced within my own adoption, came an ugly and sometimes frightening divorce between my parents. My father left and eventually started his own family elsewhere. My mother returned to her career. I was an only child, so what happened behind closed doors literally remained sealed off from anyone else.

For me this led to huge insecurity issues. I became the person I thought people wanted me to be. I "played the part" but the real me remained hidden, unidentifiable, even by me.

It was like the scenario of the princess trapped in the tall tower of a castle. I knew I wasn't meant to be there and that it wasn't my fault that I was there. All I knew was that I had to please the people holding me captive until I could find a way out or until someone came to rescue me.

The only problem was that the longer I stayed in that tower, the more urgent it became to find a way out. The walls closed in more and more each year. I found it hard to breathe. The real me seemed to be slipping into a coma, never to be heard from again, while the surface me tried to keep up some sort of appearance of whatever "normal" was.

I tried to please everyone – this included extended family, friends, teachers, coaches, etc. I was like a chameleon in that I would try to look and act like whoever was near me at the time.

In my mind, I would assess people to see what made them happy and I would say and do things that I thought would make them like me. But it seemed that no matter how hard I tried, I was never good enough. I wasn't cut out to be the type of friend others wanted. I wasn't skilled enough to excel in school or any of the groups I wanted so desperately to join. I wasn't limber enough for cheerleading. My physique wasn't delicate enough for ballet. I wasn't talented enough on my violin for the orchestra. I wasn't even capable of being a "good" daughter. I started to think maybe there was a good reason my first mother gave me up.

When I approached 16 years of age, it just got to be too much. I saw that no matter how hard I tried, I couldn't please everyone all of the time. I wanted out somehow but escape didn't seem possible anymore so my thoughts began to drift to life beyond this earth. I wanted my days in the tower to end.

I began to look for ways to end the pain I was experiencing inside. No one else knew the hell I was going through – it was all a secret. I looked at the shallowness of the kids around me at school. Who could even begin to comprehend my life?

I literally tried everything to get rid of the pain. Nothing worked. I called out to God (who else could I call out to?) I screamed into the air, "God, if you are there, you better prove yourself. Find me. Save me. Because if you don't I will end my life one way or another." I didn't hear anything.

"Great. I'm not even good enough for God to help."

Silence.

I awoke the next day and I felt something new. Don't get me wrong, the inner me was still trapped in the tower but there was a crack in the wall. It was so small, just a sliver. I couldn't identify or explain it but it was something new, something different. I wanted to grab it before it was gone. I was willing to do anything to keep that little sliver alive. Whatever it was, I wanted it. I know now that little sliver was the slightest hint of hope, something I never had before. I wasn't even sure what I was hoping for but there it was and I wasn't going to let it go.

It was after this that I began to listen to something inside of me that began to prompt me to find and follow paths that began to lead me to freedom.

However, I will mention here that as I began to find freedom, the people around me were not happy. My freedom meant that I was no longer saying and doing things that pleased them. I could no longer be contained in the tower at everyone else's bidding. I wasn't predictable anymore and this upset everyone around me. I wasn't anyone's slave and I was no longer going to put up with the abuse I had previously taken as something I deserved.

I had a new strength rising within me and I openly declared that it came from God and boy that did not go down well with anyone I previously knew. I had a feeling they thought, "She says she's following God. How do I compete with that? How do I override God to get her to do what I want her to do?" I was mocked in every way possible, especially from family members.

Yet in all of this I seemed to start seeing things more clearly. I began to learn some amazing life lessons.

In the past, I would often have horrible and vivid nightmares. I was always running and I would fall back into consciousness scared and breathing heavy. The dreams were so real and terrifying. When I prayed, I felt God leading me to stop running and to turn around and see what it was I was running from. (I never realized that I actually had control in my dreams.) I was able to stop and turn around to face what was so frightening. My nightmares stopped. I took it to another level and decided to start facing all of my fears. I learned:

Never let fear drive your decisions. Stop, turn around and face your fears, define them. Then decide if you need to run or not.

I have friends that have stuck it out and worked through their adoption issues in and amongst their family and friends but I must admit I ran and it was the best decision I have ever made. I found that the people closest to me kept trying to "fix" my issues and often would trigger old issues, bringing back what I thought I had already dealt with.

I was hurt and broken and I needed to recover before I could make any good decisions. In fact, I didn't even know if I was capable of making any decisions by myself. I was so blessed that I had friends that took me in for living arrangements for several years until I married and moved to the other side of the world! When I had the distance and no chance of interference in my life, I was able to face issues on my terms and I finally began to heal.

Be still. Learn how to listen and observe.

This is a lost art today. We are surrounded by distractions: TV, computers, iPods, mobile/cell phones, traffic, children, worries, over-commitment, and the list goes on. Many times there are paths to answers all around us but we miss them because we are so busy or distracted.

It wasn't until I learned how to be still that I learned how to listen. I found it took a long time to hear the real me buried deep down and to the voice beyond. It got to a point that one day, I said to God, "I will sit on this beach (I live near the ocean) until I hear your voice." I was committed and I stayed put. Hours ticked by and I found I was distracted by everything! The views, my memories, songs, favorite shows, etc. I could not get my brain to "shut up" so I could focus and listen. After six hours I started to see things clearly, after seven, I started to hear, to really hear.

That sounds crazy doesn't it? I mean who just sits still for that long of time? But think to yourself, what did people do before technology? Has something been lost besides time itself?

You may think that's a lot of time but really in the spectrum of life, it's nothing. I enjoyed that time so much that I remember the following year I made it a weekly thing to sit on the beach for a couple of hours to get still and it was the best year of my life.

I guess I think of it like this: if someone you loved was in a hospital, hurt or dying, you would make the time to be with them. You are someone that may be hurt or dying within! Make the time for yourself! Book it in like your life counted on it, because I believe it does.

When you go through the process of working things out, voice it!

You can talk to someone you trust, or to God or write it in a journal. Put it out there. Once it is voiced or written, you can deal with it more clearly. You can write it down and burn it up after but there is something about putting words clearly on paper in front of you that begins a healing.

Be prepared for a shock!

As soon as you start to deal with issues of any sort, you start opening doors into the unknown. You may find information about others in your family history that you never dreamed could happen (good and bad). Yet you may just uncover something about yourself that is just as shocking. When you discover something shocking, take some time to digest it before acting upon it.

I know that I am truly blessed in that I found out information about my birth family. Yet as I began to uncover my story piece by piece, there was a shocking discovery at each step. There were "secrets" everywhere from how I was conceived, to how I was adopted, things my mother hid from me, medical discoveries, sibling rivalry, affairs, deception, forgery, and much of that is still right where I discovered it.

After initially getting over the shocks, I began to put the whole picture together. I could have been angry with all of them, believe me! But as I stepped back from it all, it created a bigger story and that story was me!

As my story unfolded, it created a tapestry with light and dark, good and bad. I found at first, I was focusing on the back of the tapestry with all the knots and jumbled thread, trying to pick things apart. But as I stepped back and turned it around, it looked completely different. The longer I looked at it, I decided I didn't want to spend any more time trying to fix it. I wanted to sew in something new.

Bring things into the light (stop hiding, stuffing things down).

The only things that thrive in darkness and all the crap within it, are mushrooms. The things that you feel you "should never talk about" are usually the very things you should!

Obviously this is a process. For me, I had an eating disorder that I hid for a very long time. Since then, I have written a book and talked to thousands about this disorder but the thing that amazes me, is that in all of that time, not one person ever laughed or thought I was strange. Quite the contrary! I've had women come to me with tears streaming down their faces thanking me for saying the very things they were always afraid to share. People may not share the same experiences as you but you would be surprised how many people can relate to issues that surround your experience. Issues like abandonment, isolation, abuse and insecurity are universal.

Pick your family. You have a choice!

You can choose whom you will open up to and whom you need to keep at a distance. I have found that it is quite rare for a person to work out their issues surrounding adoption with close family members because they have completely different issues with adoption and are seeing it in a completely different way.

Like the lenses of a pair of glasses, we are all born with particular lenses that we see through. These lenses impact how we see and interpret situations and other people. A variety of things make up your lens – culture, family, tradition, friendships, education, upbringing, opinions, our past, etc. The list goes on.

Everyone views life through different lenses. So to expect other people to see things the way we do when they are looking through a different lens is really difficult, if not impossible for some. People who are not open to viewing through a lens that is different from their own will not come to a point where they see things as you do, ever.

Yet, the same can be said for you. Are you willing to see things from someone else's lenses, even if their lenses are smudged or the wrong type? What about if they are right, which is sometimes harder to accept? You don't have to take on board their views but it does help you to better form your own.

For me, this process has helped me to set boundaries with people. Knowing their lenses, I will share a certain amount in a certain way with my family as opposed to my closest friends. I also know what to receive from people I trust, and what to just let go of from people whose opinion I do not value.

Focus on the issues, not the person, because you can never change the person, but you can deal with the issues.

I learned that being angry with my parents (all of them) was only hurting me. They couldn't care less what I was thinking and wouldn't give two hoots if I was angry with them or not! I couldn't move forward because I was always stuck in the past. I decided that I can't change what happened but I can decide what I will do today. This led me to learn:

You are not your past.

Your parents and their issues do not define you. Thank God! I could have stayed in the tower and I would have been completely justified in the way I felt, abused and hurt. But was that going to help me?

I used to read the statistics of people who were abused and continued the cycle into their own families. I was never going to get married because I didn't want to experience a divorce ever again. I didn't want to have children because I didn't want to treat them the way I was treated. I had a whole list of things that I was never going to do because of my experience of the past. But thankfully, over the years, I began to trust that I could do anything with God's help. Now I have been happily married for nearly 20 years, I have four beautiful children and I love my life!

Know there are seasons.

Yes, I have learned a lot of great lessons but that doesn't mean my life is all hunky dory. What does that mean anyway?

For me, I would be happy with just summer and autumn every year. Get rid of the other two! But there they are. They come every year.

There are going to be hard times. There will be "seasons" when I am upset at what the past has done to me. There are still consequences that I have to live with today that resulted from "their" stupidity. Sometimes I need to allow my anger to come forward and I need to simmer in it for a while. Sometimes I go through a season of sorrow, grieving for missed opportunities. Yet in those times I remember it's a snowstorm and summer is coming, eventually. Enduring through those difficult seasons has helped me to appreciate just how tough I have become and that I get to decide what I will choose to take with me out of this time.

I ask myself, "Do I want to move on? Am I willing to leave this? Maybe I'll return to it one day but maybe I will not. Am I willing to let go of my feelings to take the chance to go in a new direction? Do I need to give this issue a proper burial? What can I take from this that will help me on my journey? What do I need to leave behind so I don't carry so much excess baggage?"

You are created for a purpose.

I believe every person is created for a purpose. Every person on this planet holds something unique and special to bring into this life, including me!

I am still working on what is buried deep within. I'm only just discovering in my 40's what I really want do with my life! But you know, that is okay. I still wrestle with self-confidence issues and I know that it is going to be a process, but at least I'm taking little steps in the right direction. It doesn't ever seem to look like I imagined it will but that's okay too!

I started to play the violin again. I played not so long ago in a music forum and I was told it wasn't good enough.

I also played for a group of people in an aged care program. The people told me the music was beautiful. One man had tear-filled eyes and a big smile after I played the song he requested.

I choose to keep playing.

Marla Jones was adopted at birth and raised in Centerville, Ohio. She currently lives in Perth, Western Australia with her husband Mark. They have four children; the youngest adopted from the Philippines. Marla is passionate about helping others through her experience and her faith in God. She has also written and published the book, *Hungry for Life.*

PART II: SURVIVING ADOPTIVE FAMILY RELATIONSHIPS

If you stop anyone t and ask them what their needs are, I bet they have a mental list ready right on the spot. "I need a new car." "I need a new job." "I need a new..." You get the picture. But if we all pause to think about it, we "want" those things, not need.

What we need is food, shelter, clothing, and at the least, some peace in our hearts. And yes, okay, a car would certainly make life easier for most of us and may be fun too. So what if we go deeper than that? What about needs that our souls have? That our hearts yearn for? The average person would probably respond, "Nah, I'm pretty good here. My family is near me; they have my back. I can count on their support."

If I could somehow stop myself on that street, and ask myself this question, my answer would be more like this:

"Well, I need to be accepted. I need 'connection.' I need to feel wanted. I need to feel loved. I need to be validated and my feelings validated, as well, for once in my life. Since we are getting real, I need constant reassurance that 'whoever' isn't going to leave me the first chance they get, and no matter how many times people may tell me they aren't going anywhere, I never believe them."

Here's my story. I was told I was purchased for adoption at the age of two. I was told right away. I've known since the beginning of my memory. In the beginning, it was all right; I mean I didn't really "feel" much about it, or understand it even at such a young age. I didn't know what that word meant – adopted. I remember thinking they picked me off a store shelf, like grocery shopping or something. That's kind of how they made it sound anyway. By "they" I mean my adoptive parents.

What I did know was that I was different, and particularly different from the siblings in the house of which I never felt a part of. I remember being mocked for feeling things that the others in the house didn't feel on any given subject. I really felt like I had been dropped into this family from Mars and I was from Pluto. We couldn't communicate, we didn't think alike at all, we didn't see eye to eye ever. Yet I pretended for decades since I wasn't ever given a choice in the matter anyway. Adoptees are survivors, plain and simple. As the years went on and I grew up, things only got worse.

My questions about who my real mother was, or where I came from, or where she was now, and why, why, why and why only got stronger and more weighty on my heart and soul. This did not go well with my adoptive family. I was told horrible things about my birth mother and birth father in the hopes I would then drop the whole subject. I couldn't drop it. There was something in my bones that just had to be found out and known within my very soul.

Who did I come from? Why was I given up to start with? What happened? Did I do something wrong? Is there something wrong with me, or was it that my mother just couldn't stand me? And asking these questions of my adoptive parents wasn't helpful; they chose to either not answer me at all, or give me tidbits of false information. And they lied, a lot. I didn't give up. I couldn't. Every time, my adoptive parents told me, "You have a chip on your shoulder," or "You think you're special, but your mother gave you up, let it go," or "Get over it already!"

But their words just provided me ammunition to NOT give up. I know that is backwards as hell, but their insistence on me dropping it, actually pushed me to find every piece of information that I could. My need to belong was so strong; I couldn't stop digging until I found my place on this planet.

I was 32, I think, when I found out who I was, and where I came from, and who I came from. I did it without my adoptive family's help, but with many wonderful friends and searchers online, and it took me one solid year of nonstop digging. When I started, I didn't even know who I was before adoption. Now I know.

I was one year too late finding my mother. She had passed one year before the day I found and confirmed who she was (If you need to know, then I suggest you do it now, so that maybe you can find and meet your roots before it's too late.) My need to know got me results. Not all of it is pretty; not any of it is glamorous. Both birth parents had passed by the time I found everything. But I know I have a lot of blood relatives. I got to talk to people close to my mother, and hear stories about her and her life. I had to let that be enough, since she was no longer living.

And to me, just having her name and knowing this woman birthed me, and finding out my name before adoption, made me feel whole. I had never felt that before and it was just awesome. Like ice cream sundaes and unicorns and cotton candy-on-a-cloud with warm fuzzy angels hugging-me-nonstop, kind of awesome. It was surreal and unforgettable. I sat on the floor and cried because I knew who I was for the first time in my life. I felt like the universe was whole and so was I.

To this very day, even though I do have my court records, even though I do know who I am, and who my birth family is, even though my adoptive parents were not honest with me every step of the way, the people who raised me still do not believe I found my family. They think I am crazy. They think I am lying. And they think I am nuts for not dropping it. They think I "feel" too much and that I make something out of nothing. And that I am too sensitive.

You know what? I am sensitive. I am proud to feel and to need connection. It makes me who I am. And without any of that, I would most likely have listened to my adoptive parents and dropped it years ago without getting any answers. I am proud that I am not like them. I am proud that I am stubborn, and that I don't take "no" for an answer. And if I classify as needy, then I am proud of that too! My adoptive family and I don't speak today.

My survival tips are:

1. Listen to your gut. It is ok to need to know. It's in your basic DNA as a human even before you know who you come from. Listen to that "pull" inside you, and go for it.

2. Be brave; you only live once. If you base all decisions on what another wants or needs, you will never feel whole. Take a risk and start digging.

3. Music is my therapy. I know it's dorky, but music can heal. It can encourage, it can give you a boost of kickass you didn't previously have. It can comfort, or help you get your rage out. Use it.

4. Stand up for yourself, and for what you believe in. Your feelings count. Feelings are not debatable. If you feel it, it's real and nobody can undo that. Own your feelings; embrace them, whatever IT is that you feel.

5. Find adoptees to share with and talk to. In some way or another, we have all been there and done that, and felt that, and said that, and cried that. You are not alone.

Ann Martin was adopted at the age of 2, in the state of Texas. Today she is married, has two daughters, one cat, and two dogs. Ann and her husband live and work on a cattle ranch. She loves to write, play Boggle, and music is her personal therapy.

Always the Last to Know

by Jeff Hancock

Have you ever wondered why,
families keep secrets until they die?
This completely takes over who you are,
carving within you an unbearable scar.

The day I learned that my parents had lied,
the soul within me stopped living, and died.
I felt as though I had just lost my very best friend,
Who was I now? Was I at my start, or at my end?

I found a quote soon after I learned that I was adopted. It reads,

"The worst thing about being lied to
is knowing you weren't worth the truth."

This quote became my motto as I embarked on my new life as an adoptee. My story is quite complicated at times; it has been just over seven years since my discovery, though it still stings as though it were yesterday. I will attempt to reveal how I have faced the task of being an LDA (Late Discovery Adoptee), though I am still far from the end of my journey.

All my life I have felt a strange absence. It was a feeling of loneliness and loss. I never could quite find the right words to explain these feelings; I always just figured I was an outcast due to being so much younger than the other kids in our family. I had no idea that I could be an adoptee until I began school in 1970. It was on the bus that kids bullied me by calling me "foster kid." I brushed it off at first because as a five year old kid, I had no idea what it meant.

As I grew older, I began to take notice of how my family regarded me. I had learned what a "foster kid" was, and I began to wonder if at any time someone would tell me I was only a guest and that another family was coming to take me away.

Evidence began to surface. I was not included in my paternal grandmother's family Bible. That same grandmother never provided me with a hand sewn quilt as she had for each of her other grandchildren. Then there was the photograph. It was a Polaroid of me when I was about two years old. On the back of it was written, "Jeff, our foster son."

By the time I was 21 years old, I could not tolerate my internal struggle over my identity any longer. Having grown tired of pussy-footing around the topic with my parents, I threw my cards onto the table, called my parents, and asked, "Am I adopted?" It could not have gone any worse. Dad yelled, mom cried. Both told me that I was wrong for questioning my relationship to them. Both lied to me and told me I was theirs.

For the first year after my discovery, I walked the Earth in "zombie mode." While I was mostly aware of the goings-on around me, I was detached from it all. I took no pleasure doing things that before had brought me great joy. I had no idea who I was; I felt betrayed, rejected, unwanted, and unworthy of anyone's love. I sought solutions to my emptiness and pain. There were none.

The first time I turned on the radio in my car following the discovery, I heard a song that I had not before experienced. It was "Mother" written by Roger Waters of Pink Floyd. This new-to-me version was sung by Sinead O'Connor. I instantly became engrossed in it. I immediately bought the album. I played this song repeatedly every day for the next five-and-a-half years.

There was one line from the lyrics of "Mother" that has run through my mind over and over again since my discovery. It's the verse where a mother bird vows to keep her baby concealed under her wing. While she might later let the baby bird sing, she will never allow it to fly out on its own.

As a Late Discovery Adoptee, this verse represents a paradox for me. It symbolizes first how our government believes it is protecting us by hiding our identity; our natural desire to sing and fly like the other birds. It also symbolizes my adoptive family, who kept me hidden away for as long as they could out of fear that perhaps I would sing or fly too differently than the birds from their own flock. Rather than be truthful with me for the bird I was born to be, they clipped my wings by denying me the truth of my identity.

This became my theme song. With each passing day, I grew more and more resentful of my adoptive parents. I also grew angry with my other mom; the one who gave me away.

While I began my search for family the very same day as my discovery, by 2009, I had no more information than I had the day I began. I realized that if I were to ever find my family, I would need to have access to my original birth certificate first. I fell into the ranks of the adoptee rights movement.

My first adoptee rights protest was in Philadelphia during July of 2009. It became one of my favorite life experiences. Like how Moses must have felt delivering the Jews to the Promised Land, I too felt I had finally landed right where I belonged. As we met each other in and around the hotel over those four days, I realized that although we each had different jobs and came from different kinds of families, we were all exactly the same within our souls. We each were denied our souls.

When asked how I survived my late discovery adoption, I drew a complete blank. I wondered, "Have I survived?" At least in the eyes of my fellow adoptees, and the moms who gave birth to us, I appear to be a survivor. Within my mind, I have reservations. I am not convinced that adoption is survivable; it affects each of us for our entire lives.

Perhaps I can best offer some suggestions on how to cope with being a Late Discovery Adoptee.

Find a theme song. It seems every LDA has one. For me it was Sinead O'Connor's "Mother." For one of my friends it was "Angel" by Sarah McLachlan. While I listened to this song daily, I found it meant the most to me when I was in a long hot bath alone with my thoughts and a few candles.

Be sure to share your story. Revealing yourself to others in the adoptee community is a daunting task. It was the first time in my life that I felt genuine fear. I felt unworthy of having friendships with other adoptees. I was new to the scene while they had known all of their lives. Surprisingly, I was immediately embraced – not only by fellow LDAs – but likewise, from the entire adoption community.

I took a vow the day I found out my truth. I pledged to live my adopted life with one-hundred-percent transparency. My adoption experience is something I decided was not to be my shame, but rather my triumph.

I have met fellow adoptees, as well as original moms and dads, who accepted me for who I am. They have become my family over these years. When I found my birth families, my community through adoption welcomed and included them.

While our lives as LDAs were shrouded in secrecy and lies, our stories belong to us. We need to reveal ourselves to others in our world. Perhaps one day there will be enough awareness of our pain and our plight that lies within adoption will finally grind to a halt. Until that time comes, we must always support each other and freely share ourselves.

Jeff Hancock

In 2007, I was nearing my 42nd birthday when I discovered that I was adopted. Discovery came through the application process for a U.S. passport. It has since evolved into a non-ending search for self. My search began the same afternoon that I learned of my adoption and took six years to complete.

If the trauma of being a Late Discovery Adoptee wasn't enough, add in the shock of being denied the truth of my original identity by New York State law. That was the turning point of my life when I joined the fight for restored Original Birth Certificate access for all adoptees.

My purpose as an adoptee rights activist is to call upon all adoptees, our families (both birth and adoptive), our children, our siblings, our spouses, lawmakers, and agencies that currently provide adoption services, to unite in support of "The Adoptee Bill of Rights." Besides my volunteer activist role, I busy myself with collecting things including Buffalo Sabres hockey cards, 1/64 scale vehicles, and celebrity autographs. I'm also an avid photographer, artist, and gardener.

The Replacement Doll

by JoAnne Bennett

"Once you discover your true worth, walking away from
where you are not valued will become the easiest hard
thing you will ever do." – Stace Morris

I fondly remember when my mother gave me her childhood doll. Mom and I never had much in common. I always felt we didn't bond because I was adopted. This cherished possession from her childhood was the most meaningful gift she ever gave me.

The delicate doll needed to be handled with care; she wasn't like my other toys. I treasured my newly acquired keepsake, even when its fragile face and legs began to crack and peel from being well loved.

When I held this precious looking baby with the glistening, blue eyes and soiled white cloth body, I felt as if I was holding a part of my mother close to my heart. I longed to know its sentimental value, why this doll had been her favorite. It seemed, though, that my mother had thrown away the key to her locked diary filled with her secret childhood memories.

I unexpectedly learned of its fate one day as I placed some trash in our outside garbage can. As I looked into that dark and filthy place, I saw my doll's beautiful, blue eyes staring up at me. Cracked eggshells and soggy coffee grounds covered her body. I couldn't even hold her one last time. My heart broke.

My mother's reason for throwing it away was cold and insensitive. She was tired of mending the dirty cloth body with its stuffing falling out. I wondered why she didn't seem to show any feelings for our doll. She acted as though I cried over spilt milk. My mother was not a woman you could plead with to change her mind.

I tried to forget about this priceless gift that brought a short-lived bond with my mother. Regretfully, I couldn't fix our broken relationship. She had thrown away the one thing that connected me to her. I had her doll only for a short time, but for me, it was like holding onto a tattered, old baby blanket that had become even more special with age.

Many years ago, I received a Christmas present from her – a brand-new, expensive, 125-year anniversary doll, a look-alike to the one she had discarded. I felt an agonizing void; I needed her to give me something of herself. Through my tears, I tried to pretend that it was the most thoughtful gift. The painful truth was that we never truly understood what the other one desired.

Dressed in a long, white, christening gown, the flawless replica of the old doll sits on the bottom shelf of my curio cabinet. I don't know why I display her gift in my living room. While others admire the beautiful showpiece, all I feel is emptiness.

Mom couldn't have any more babies; I was her replacement doll. Perhaps what we did have in common were our feelings of loss. My replacement doll didn't have the same significance of what real means to me either.

To mom, I could never take the place of a biological child. Just as her extravagant, superficial gesture could never replace that precious-looking baby with the glistening, blue eyes and soiled, cloth body.

* * *

As an adoptee, when you are placed with a new family, realistically, it's not possible that every child and mother will always bond with one another. The truth is that you can't make anyone love you, including your birth or adoptive parents.

When my adoptive mother's only biological child felt the need to share with me, "Mom said she should have never adopted children because she couldn't love them as her own," I felt oddly relieved. No matter how painful the truth, what I had known since I was a little girl wasn't all in my head anymore.

> "Allow yourself to grieve the losses. This is important. You did not lose something you had. You are losing the hope of something that never happened." – Daniel J. Tomasulo, Psychologist, Professor, Trainer and Author

Sometimes, what hurts us the deepest, has more to do with other people's fears and shortcomings, rather than who we are as human beings.

It wasn't until recent years that I would even admit that my late adoptive mother had been verbally abusive, but I would always follow it up by stating she was not physically or sexually abusive. I didn't realize until recent years that there was another abuse that has caused me by far the most harm and damage: emotional abuse.

My two father figures, my oldest sibling, my relatives, and even in a sense, the state where I was born, and my birth parents, had all let me down. No one protected me from this woman's abuse. It wasn't until I found an article online about emotional abuse that I could begin to make any sense of the losses.

> "Because the abuser suffers from internal discomfort and conflicts they don't know how to address, no amount of logic, submissiveness or kindness will be enough to compensate or satisfy their insecurities. They are not seeking to understand or respect others because they do not fully understand or respect themselves. They hide from their own weaknesses by trying to make others weak. They can't control their own emotions, so they look to control others.
>
> While they may have some positive qualities, they hold toxic and unrealistic expectations which cannot be met. Those who try to meet these expectations will end up feeling like a failure because it is a game they cannot win." Signs of Emotional Abuse and How to Stop Being Victimized. (n.d.). In Designed Thinking. Retrieved Oct. 25, 2014 from designedthinking.com/thesignsofemotionalabuse.

For the longest time, I have wrestled with knowing if finding forgiveness would be easier if I could say out loud that the abuser was flawed, broken, or suffered from mental health issues. I always feared that if I dared to whisper that difficult word, "forgiveness," I would be letting my guard down with my mother, and that she somehow could hurt me again, even after she passed away.

Years ago, on one of Oprah's shows, she had shared with her viewers that a guest's definition of forgiveness was the most beneficial to her. It helped change my perspective as well. The guest said,

"When defining forgiveness, it really means letting go of the past we thought we wanted. Forgiveness is giving up the hope that the past could be any different."

Some insightful advice I ran across will take time for me to process, but could be a meaningful part of closure for those adoptees who have experienced tough adoption issues too:

"When you are stuck in knowing how to let go of the past, you should think of this huge garbage bag," says Dr. Susanna McMahon, who wrote the book, The Portable Therapist.

She suggests that one open the bag and sort through it, and that we "honor all of our past," but put back in the bag only what we need in order to go on in the present. To do this, the author stated,

"You must stop trying to make the past something it was not. If you were abused or rejected or unloved in the past, you can stop being abused, rejected, and unloved now so that you can start recovering from the guilt, fear, anxiety and depression that you might associate with these events."

"There's a difference between giving up and letting go. Giving up is sacrificing what was rightfully yours and letting go is forgetting what never was." – source unknown

The harsh reality, and what shouldn't stay in my huge garbage bag, is the replacement doll that had no significance to my adoptive mother.

From the beautiful Pacific Northwest, **JoAnne Bennett** has raised three wonderful daughters alongside her supportive husband of almost 40 years. Although her adoption journey has been difficult, she loves focusing on her passion – writing. Painfully transparent through her words, as an author her heart-felt desire is to reach others whose voices have been silenced by abuse and adoption issues, and to send the message to not feel so alone.

A poignant lesson that comes from her personal triumphs: "Never give up on discovering your gifts." JoAnne's work has appeared in print and in a number of publications over the years. She felt such a strong sense of community with her participation in The Adoptee Survival Guide.

JoAnne's most recent contribution is making a difference in the lives of young people through the anthology, *Dear Wonderful You: Letters to Adopted & Fostered Youth.*

A Plea to Adoptive Parents

by Lucy Chau Lai-Tuen

"Since I was five, I've known that I was adopted, which is a politically correct term for being clueless about one's own origins" – Jodi Picoult

"I am a cultural Frankenstein. I have no definable history before I was abandoned and taken in by the orphanage in Hong Kong. I was truly a blank sheet. I have been disconnected from my ancestors. I don't know who they are, where they came from or whether any of their line still exists. The ancestral umbilical cord that would have connected me to my past and linked me to my future was permanently severed. It cannot be reattached." – Lucy Chau Lai-Tuen

For the majority of my life I have felt invalidated by society, many of the people who work in the same industry sector that I do and the people that adopted me, not out of malice, but because in 60s pre-multicultural Britain race, ethnicity and identity had no place. Britain was white, non-diverse and was unconcerned with the identity of the relatively small number of peoples from the British colonies.

I was not told that I had been adopted. As a transracial adoptee, to a white Anglo Saxon family, it didn't take long for me to realize that I was "different" – that there was something not quite right about me in relationship to the family and those in the immediate community around me. I was the odd one out. I was the elephant in the room.

I can now talk freely about this and laugh. In fact, I've even written a one woman play based on the experiences of transracial adoptees in the UK including my own experiences of growing up in pre-multicultural, white dominated 60s Britain. The play is funny (well portions of it are).

How long did my adoptive parents think that they could keep my adoption a secret? Did it not occur to them that I would spot the physical differences?

Seriously, I was a Chinese child in a white family growing up in the heart of Conservative (Republican) England? Need I say more?

In the 60s, the accepted method of dealing with adoption was the "clean break." While that might work for same race adoptions or Eurocentric adoptions, for the transracially adopted, (crossing racial groups and ethnicities) it was never going to "work."

The more my adoptive parents refused to talk to me about where I had come from and why I was here, the more I pushed. That's what children do, isn't it? They push the boundaries to understand their limitations. That's how we learn about wrong and right, morality, how society works and what is expected of you.

The more I challenged, the more my adoptive parents clammed up and closed ranks. The older I got, the further away I grew from them and the more isolated I felt from family and the wider society. My adoption was a verboten topic. Therefore, I fought tooth and nail for knowledge about who and what I was. This caused problems pretty early on, though neither my adoptive parents nor I were probably aware of that at the time.

In my opinion (and with hindsight), they didn't want to face the fact that they knew absolutely nothing about raising a non-white child. They had no knowledge or understanding of the country or culture that I had been born into. Zero experience of foreign travel and as far as I am aware, no interaction with other central Europeans, let alone East Asians.

As a six-year-old child, I had very little sense of who or what I was. But I was aware from a very early age that I didn't look the same as the other members of the family. This was odd because all the other families that I saw all looked like each other. I had a flat nose and oddly shaped eyes, which prompted people to pull faces at me and shout at me in a strange fake Chinese accent.

So I tried to alter my appearance at a very early age. I would go to bed with an old fashioned wooden clothes peg on my nose. In my infantile naivety, I thought that doing this would elongate and straighten my nose giving me the bridge that was missing, and the classic roman-nosed profile. I taped my eyes open before I went to sleep, hoping that this would widen my eyes and make them look more like everyone else's.

Even with the advanced technology of the 21st century, unless you have considerable financial resources, you cannot easily change the physical attributes that your race and ethnicity has handed down to you. So back in the relative dark-ages of the 60s, how I thought I could change my physical appearance, Lord only knows. But then I was only six (probably younger) when I started trying to change my appearance. I just wanted to fit in. To look like everyone else. Isn't that what every child wants, to be like everyone else and not to stand out?

As a transracial adoptee, physical likeness and the ability to see my reflection through the eyes, faces of my parents and other members of the family, was never going to happen. I was never going to see my future self, as most children do, through their parents' likeness. I would never catch a glimpse of what I might grow up to look like. I think it is imperative for adoptive parents to take responsibility and ensure that the child they transracially adopt is told about the circumstances of that adoption. The whys, the wheres and the hows.

By taking those steps as soon as possible, you acknowledge that the child has a history that is all their own. That it is as valuable to the parents as it is to the child. It demonstrates the parents' understanding and appreciation of the child. It validates the child and their experience.

I have heard many adoptive parents say to their children after they have been racially abused, "Oh, it's nothing" or "It doesn't matter" or worse still, "they didn't mean anything by it". I have lost count of the times that I have heard these types of responses from adoptive parents. I don't mix very often with adoptive parents, but when I hear these responses, that, in and of itself, says something that we as a society need to take on board.

Many adoptive parents shrug off these playground incidents as "nothing". Well, if it were "nothing," if it didn't mean anything, then the child wouldn't have told you. What does this say to the adopted child? It is saying that part of them – the ethnic part, the coloured or the different cultural part – doesn't matter. It has no place in this new world. The world that their adoptive parents are trying to shoe horn them into. A world which usually tends to be white and privileged.

We all need to know where we come from and how we fit into our family and the wider society. If you're adopted this can be complicated. If you're transracially adopted then it becomes more than just complicated. We in part define ourselves by our sameness to the family that we come from, whilst at the same time, it is accepted that we are unique. If you are a naturally born child, you have a family, ancestors and roots. You can trace and tap into your lineage. You can literally see your path – the line – that runs through time and ancestors.

You can follow an unbroken connection. It shows you where you came from and who you are. If you're like me and have no connection, either physically or culturally, then you will always be challenged. By those on the outside, those close to you and more importantly by yourself. You will always be searching for validation. I grew up in a white dominated community during a time when non-white people were the exception and not the rule.

Non-white people appearing in public, on TV, or as public figures, were the exception. Society saw me as the "other," the "foreigner," "the outsider." I was marked out for being different, for not being like everyone else. I never felt validated. I still don't to this day feel entirely validated as a human being. For many people, including my adoptive parents, I don't think I existed in the same sense that they did. Physically I was different to everyone else which made me abnormal. Society didn't see my experiences or me in the same way. In fact, my experiences were not valid because I was not like them.

The ability to see and understand where you come from, for the majority, is taken for granted. But it enables you to gain a sense of belonging on a personal and interpersonal level, on the micro and macro scheme of things. In other words, your very existence is given credence. If you cannot tap into this network of history, culture and linguistics, finding your place in life can be an extreme challenge.

For a so-called human construct, identity is a very powerful idea, and one that people all over the globe adhere to. It is the core of what "needing to know" for an adoptee is all about. It is as essential as the act of breathing is. An involuntary, emotional need, which we cannot switch off.

Being open and honest with the child that you have adopted means that you care. You understand the importance of the child's life before the adoption. It also says to the child that you're not afraid of the child's life before, with another family, perhaps in another country with a different history, culture and language.

If adoptive parents can accept and embrace that part of the child, then the world is your oyster. If adoptive parents can accept the child in his entirety and not just cherry-pick the bits of the child that they feel most comfortable with, then the family will go from strength to strength.

Adoptive parents have to be confident, comfortable and humble enough to be able to cope with all the challenges that raising a transracially adopted child might have in store for them.

How many times have I heard adoptive parents in the UK say that the past doesn't matter. Or we'll tell them, maybe later. Or they don't really need to know, as long as we love the child. Which in many of the cases that I have personally come across, is a love that is expressed via things, material objects, not by emotions, actions or thoughts.

I can say with confidence that "love" is not enough. There certainly has to be love in any relationship, be that familial or otherwise. Unconditional love. Tough love. As adoptive parents to a transracially adopted child, you have to have a whole battery of other things in your parental armory. You must understand the racial dynamics and politics of the country that you're bringing the child up in. You must understand the true nature of diversity and cultural sensitivity, and be able to offer the child a complete set of social and cultural tools, so that they can manage the diverse and sometimes negative situations that they will undoubtedly encounter, because of their skin colour, the texture of their hair or the shape of their eyes.

As adoptive parents now more so than when I was adopted, you are going to be battered and bruised by emotions, challenges, questions and ignorant people. Many of whom don't realise what they're doing or saying. Many of whom don't understand that their actions are hurtful and damaging to the transracially-adopted child. As a parent, you have to be able to withstand this battery not only from the outside but also from within, from family members and from the child.

You cannot take what a child says personally. You have to have the generosity of spirit and emotional maturity to listen and take on board those difficult questions from the child. Remember this is never about you, the adoptive parent; it is always about the child. Never make this about you because if you do you'll lose every time.

The need to know does not dissipate with age. In my case it grew stronger and stronger as the years ticked by. For a very, very, very long time I ignored this need to know, burying it deep. Trying to get on with my life. Going through a hollow set of daily motions. But it doesn't matter how deep you try to bury this desire, in the end, it will always resurface.

It's not just a question of if, but when. If you're in denial when you finally face whatever it is you were running away from the "it" always seems to have grown, the challenge greater and larger than it originally was.

My need to know has been responsible for me coming to terms with who I am. Of embracing the contradictions and the challenges. Of finally being comfortable in my own skin. I no longer worry or concern myself with other people's opinions of what they think I should be or ought to be, because of the way I look or the way that I sound over the phone, or because of my name and the subconscious assumptions that people make. The need to know is primal, instinctive, guttural and hardwired into the DNA of each and every one of us.

I would love to know where I came from. Whether I look like my mother, or have my father's eyes or my grandmother's nose. I will never look on the face of my own kin, ever. This does not lessen my desire to find my ancestral location. To know for certain where I sit and how I fit into the world. The desire does not decrease because I do not know and am never likely to know who my parents were. If anything, it rages all the brighter and harder because of that very fact.

I will keep searching. I will continue to talk out loud in public as a recovering transracial adoptee and I will continue to write. It's through my work that I discover each day more about me and the connection to my birth parents, and culture. I will never see my mother's face. But through me, my ancestors continue to live. I honor my birth mother's sacrifice with each play, each poem that I write and each breath that I take. I come closer to an understanding and the need to know with every work that I pen. In the end, it is me that validates my own life by continuing to live and share my life views through my writing.

Lucy Sheen – stage name, nom de plume Lucy Chau Lai-Tuen: made in Hong Kong and exported to the UK as a transracial adoptee. Lucy is a dyslexic actor, published writer, filmmaker, trainer and transracial adoptee advocate. She loves Dim sum, Yorkshire puddings and tea.

Her first professional job was the female lead in a British feature film PING PONG (1987), directed by Po Ch'ih Leong. The first ever UK feature to look at the history and issues of the British-Chinese community.

Other publications that Lucy has contributed to: *Dear Wonderful You: Letters to Fostered and Adopted Youth*; *Adoption Therapy: Perspectives from Clients and Clinicians on Processing and Healing Post-Adoption Issues*; *Adoptionland: From Orphan to Activist*; and *Perpetual Child: Adult Adoptee Anthology: Dismantling the Stereotype*.

Lucy is also in post-production for her independent documentary: *Abandoned, Adopted Here* – a film that looks at what identity and belonging means to a transracial adoptee growing up in pre multicultural 60s Britain.

You may visit Lucy at www.lucysheen.com.

Relative Strangers

by Jodi Haywood

"Is that your grandma?"

I was probably ten years old, playing in the basement with a neighborhood friend and a couple of her friends, all younger than me. My adoptive mother had come downstairs to talk to us, briefly, and was on her way back up the creaky wooden steps when one of the girls asked the question.

I shook my head, too embarrassed to speak. I could have said she was my mom, but I knew I was adopted, so that explanation felt less than true to me. On the other hand, I didn't know all of these girls, and we didn't tell "strangers" about my adoption. But the word "mom" didn't entirely fit the woman raising me, who at 45 years my senior could easily have been my grandma. In the early to mid-1980s, nobody else's mother wore her hair up in a bun with a scarf wrapped around it – if it were any taller, it could have passed for a beehive. Her clothes were as outdated as her hairdo. Between that and her proper British accent, she embarrassed me. Once in a while someone would tell me I looked a bit like her, and I dismissed those comments with the scorn they deserved. I was adopted. Adopted meant that I had no biological connection to this aging couple who'd taken me into their home and insisted on calling themselves my "parents". Didn't it?

"Am I an orphan?" I asked her once, soon after seeing Annie on one of the rare occasions she took me to the movies. Her idea of good entertainment involved the ballet or symphony orchestra, or a "literary" play. I knew next to nothing about popular culture, but she had taken me to Annie, and something about that red-haired orphan girl daydreaming about her parents, waiting for them to come back and get her – it threatened to touch a place I'd kept locked away inside me for longer than I could remember.

"No, you're not an orphan."

"Where are my parents?" I might have said "real parents". I can't quite remember. She refused to divulge any information. I'd never been adept at picking up on nonverbal cues, although there was this unspoken understanding that she preferred not to talk about my adoption or the life it had replaced.

"Where did I come from? Where did you get me?" I'd read enough about adoption to know that agencies placed children. I knew I'd come from England; my British citizenship was impossible to hide, unlike the accent I had worked hard to lose in second grade. One of the many things that set me apart from my classmates. I also knew that my adoptive mother had brought me over herself. She'd told me about the plane ride with her and her own mother, who'd gone back to England after some time. But again I never got a straight answer.

"The Daisy Hill Puppy Farm" was the only explanation she gave me, until I turned twelve. That's where Snoopy came from, in the Peanuts comics, and I still remember reading the episode where Snoopy set out to find his old home, only to find the Daisy Hill Puppy Farm gone.

You really can't ever go back home.

By sixth grade I was reading every adoption story I could find at the library or the local secondhand bookstore. Most of the stories turned out the same. The adopted character found her birth mother, or at least discovered her identity, and went back to her adoptive parents and lived happily ever after. I wrote my own story in which a girl discovered she was adopted and ran away to live with her real parents, who welcomed her with open arms.

Not the most logical plot ever, but it speaks volumes about my relationship to my adopters, how closely I had (not) bonded to them. I was eleven, acting out in school, seeing a psychologist – and my main topic of conversation during those sessions with him was my adoption. Who was I, where did I come from, and who were my real parents? I was much more interested in connecting with my father than my mother.

I think it was a combination of the good doctor's influence and the proposed trip to England for my twelfth summer that brought the truth out. My adoptive mother – and this is the last time I would think of her as such – started by showing me a British passport with a baby's photograph and her own maiden name.

Despite my confusion, I figured it must have meant we were related somehow. Maybe she really was my grandmother. That's when I discovered that the man I'd always written to as "Uncle George" was my father.

I'd always wanted to meet "Uncle" George, my adopter's younger brother, who'd moved back to England after spending some years in Bermuda with his wife. He had a German shepherd, and I longed for a dog even more than the sister or brother the adopters refused to give me. (I figured if they adopted once, they could adopt twice, but she always said "one is enough".) I'd been excited about seeing him – and his dog – since we started planning the trip to England. Finding out he was my dad felt like a birthday present and a practical joke at the same time. I tried to call the adopters "aunt" and "uncle," as they were, but they expected me to act as if this new information didn't change a thing for me, and instructed me not to tell any of my friends.

I told them anyway. As happy as I was to learn the truth, I felt betrayed, shaken to the core, like everything I ever believed about myself was a lie. What was wrong with simply telling me the truth from the beginning and letting me grow up calling them what they really were? Why not let me keep my own place in the family instead of trying to replace my parents? I wanted to know why my parents hadn't kept me, since Dad and his wife, Linda, seemed to have a fairly normal life. Why did they give me away? Why didn't they ever come back for me? Then there was the huge letdown that I didn't have a whole other family separate from the adopters. I'd been with relatives all along and not known it.

And my grandmother! She'd visited every year for my birthday, flown in from England with a suitcase full of candy, and made me miserable well into summer vacation. My birthday came soon before school got out, so we always went camping for a week or so in my uncle's old VW van. I loathed camping almost as much as I despised my grandmother. I can't put my finger on what it was I didn't like about her, but we never had a warm fuzzy relationship.

In every photo I have, I'm standing about as far from her as I can, with my hands behind my back or clasped somehow to avoid touching her. In the earlier pictures where she's holding on to me, I look as if I'm trying to escape. Yet my adoptive mother always told me to be nice to my grandmother because "she's the only one you've got."

This made no sense to me. I was adopted, wasn't I? I had to have two real grandmothers out there, somewhere. And if this woman wasn't my real mother, her mom couldn't be my real grandmother, right? She was just one more part of the "family" I didn't belong to. Grandma died when I was nine, and I felt nothing. Even when I saw how much my adoptive mother missed her, I only felt relief that she wouldn't be back to visit anymore.

All these birthdays she showed up for, all the camping trips, and I never knew she was my real grandmother. My most vivid memory of her was probably her last visit. I must have been eight. The three of us – me, my aunt, and her – flew to Disneyland. Alone with her in the motel room for a short time, she told me she didn't like me anymore. I can't remember what I said or did – I was acting out somehow – but that stuck in my mind.

Maybe I should have some regrets, but I don't. My aunt and uncle – but especially my aunt – should have been honest with me from the beginning. Telling me I was adopted, but not giving me the entire story, wasn't honest. Making me call them "mom" and "dad" – instead of letting me choose what felt right to me – was not honest either. My uncle was never "dad" to me, and since that day I've called him by his first name. My aunt would have either slapped me or sent me on a guilt trip around the world had I called her anything but "mom," even in reunion with my own mother.

When I met my dad, we bonded instantly. Knowing what I do now, all we did was strengthen an existing bond that my aunt had tried to pull apart. My visit with him was much too short – only a few days – but he felt like Dad to me. He felt like home. I wanted to stay.

The shocks didn't end there. Since he was my dad, I naturally assumed "Aunt" Linda was my mom. I believed this until late one night when I heard voices from downstairs and found Dad, Linda, my aunt and uncle digging through old family photos. I let Dad invite me into the gathering and looked through pictures of him and my two aunts (one had died at 17, decades before I was born), and other relatives. My grandmother had actually been pretty in her younger days; I'd never have recognized her. I saw nothing of myself in her, though. Dad showed me a picture of his first wife, and then a young blond woman in a pink outfit, holding a small baby. "That's your mother."

I looked at the photo, then at Linda, seeing no resemblance at all.

When the awkward silence had passed, I realized this blond woman, not Linda, had given birth to me. Who – and where – was she? Another, earlier photo told me her hair was a natural reddish brown, close to my own color, and I saw a faint resemblance. I learned her name. I also learned I had two half-siblings from her previous marriage and asked my dad to help me find them.

It's been nearly 30 years since that summer, and I never have located my sister or brother. My mother doesn't know where they are, either. I reunited with her on my 26th birthday and learned I'd been told a few lies and half-truths by my dad and stepmother. I'd often wondered why she hadn't contacted me the summer she attempted to track down my siblings; I was 16, and Dad wrote to my aunt to tell her she showed up out of the blue to enlist his aid in finding them. I figured if she wanted to get in touch with her "lost children," she might write me too, but no letter came. My aunt said by way of explanation, "You're not lost to her." But I wasn't exactly found, either. I pretended it didn't bother me, but my anger came out in other ways that summer – and afterward.

It turns out that my dad had told her not to contact me because I hated her.

Relative adoption. It's sort of like being a divorced kid, only you don't get to live with either of your parents.

My aunt died in January 2010. I went through her filing cabinet and took out all the files pertaining to me, including my psychiatric records from early childhood – and some letters written, separately, by both of my parents. For some reason I didn't notice the letters until after my 40th birthday, after reading The Primal Wound by Nancy Verrier and realizing the extent to which adoption had inflicted its trauma upon me.

I believe God reveals things to us as we are ready to receive them. The letter from my mother, dated 1976, protested the adoption and asked my aunt to please consider any alternatives she could. She resisted signing the papers to relinquish me. She wanted to see me that summer, if my grandmother could bring me with her when she returned to England after my birthday visit, and have another chance at raising me. She suggested that once I was old enough to make a decision, I could choose for myself who I wanted to live with. Finally, she hoped to be able to keep in touch with me.

Apparently my aunt made that choice for me, as she had made other choices that forever altered the course of my life. I don't know how she coerced my parents into signing the relinquishment papers when neither of them wanted to. In fact, my father accused her of humiliating him, which caused – or at least contributed to – the strain on their relationship for the rest of their lives. Suffice it to say I never got to choose who I wanted to live with, or even to spend summer vacations with my mother. I never received mail from her or an address I could write to her at, not until I was 25 and had already grown up without a mother.

After fifteen years in reunion with my mother, I've only just learned the entire truth about my adoption. I was never given up. I was neither abandoned nor relinquished. My mother entrusted my father's parents with my temporary care, until she was in a better position to look after me. She'd gone to her own parents in Northern Ireland, near Armagh during the time of the Troubles in the mid-1970s, and my father and his parents considered it an unsafe place for me.

When my grandfather died and my grandmother made the choice not to care for me any longer, nobody let my mother know. Instead, my aunt – who suffered from infertility and desperately wanted children, a fact hidden from me during her lifetime – took matters into her own hands and decided I could become the child she was unable to conceive. After taking me out of my homeland and separating me from my parents by thousands of miles, she made a formal application to adopt me. My father had a criminal record and my mother was a single woman recovering from an abusive relationship. Neither one was in any position, financially, legally or emotionally, to put up much of an argument, but my mother pleaded with my aunt to allow her some relationship with me. She wanted to stay in contact, to be involved in my life as my real mother, to have me know the truth – which my paternal grandmother allegedly promised her I would.

The adoption was finalized the year after my mother penned that letter.

Relative adoptions are nothing new. For as long as young girls have gotten pregnant out of wedlock, family members have stepped in to raise their babies as their own. Grandmothers have passed off their daughters' children as their own to save face in the community, and mother becomes the "older sister", often going on to raise a family that doesn't include the illegitimate grandchild. Aunts, uncles, and older married siblings or cousins might take the baby to raise, usually making arrangements prior to its birth. Teen girls would go away to visit an "aunt" or "sister" in another town and come back with their shame transferred out of sight.

Not all of these guardianship arrangements are legal adoptions. Historically, birth certificates may have been falsified to conceal the child's illegitimate status. Grandchildren raised as their mothers' younger siblings might never have learned the truth about their origins; after all, the biological connection to both guardians still existed, providing the genetic mirroring so necessary to child development and discouraging any questions that the child might not be their own.

On the other hand, the "primal wound" caused by early separation from the natural mother would also exist, manifesting itself in various ways depending on how close the child's relationship was to the true mother.

An aunt and uncle adoption, such as I had, or another relative adoption would provide biological connection on one side, but not the other – similar to a child with one natural parent and one stepparent, but again, not denying the effect of maternal separation. The child may bond with the blood relative and resent the "outsider," creating a stepparent-like dynamic, or find an attachment figure separate from the family, who has no relational bias.

The soul-deep wound created at the time of separating a baby or child from its natural mother is no less profound when the "replacement mother" is a member of the natural family. A baby or toddler can enjoy a family gathering, passed around from Grandma to Aunt to Great-Aunt with little or no fuss at first, but the time will come when Mom and only Mom can meet the youngster's needs and soothe his or her anxiety. Preventing Mom from doing so, especially if she is still present in the family, will create confusion and frustration for the child. Adopted or fostered children, in the absence of maternal comfort, will almost certainly develop self-soothing behavioral patterns and may resist the comfort of strangers – that is, anyone other than the natural mother.

The problems inherent in "guardianship adoption" are no different to those in "stranger adoption". As long as the birth certificate is falsified, using names other than the child's own parents, the child is separated from his or her natural caregivers and loses his or her rightful place in the family. Whether it is the natural mother's twin sister or an unrelated stranger on the other side of the world, the woman raising the baby "as her own" is no less a separate entity than the woman who carried and nurtured the baby inside her for nine months, give or take.

When there is no natural parent able or willing to care for the child, a family guardianship agreement is obviously preferable to the child being relinquished to strangers. The child still has an opportunity to know at least one side of his or her family, including the vitally important medical history. One would expect the related caregivers to be more sympathetic to the child who has lost his or her natural parents, either to abandonment or death, and give the child time and space to grieve.

The child could have access to, or contact with, both parents if they are still living. In the best of circumstances, the child would have the benefit of extended family to surround them with love, understanding, and nurture. This type of scenario would make legal adoption unnecessary.

In a perfect world, adoption would not be necessary at all. Every child would have one or both natural parents to love them, raise them, care for them. But families fall apart, parents become ill, parents die, and other caregivers are needed to take the child in. Every child needs a home. The fact is, though, parents are not replaceable or interchangeable, and every child deserves to know where he or she came from.

Everyone deserves the truth about their origins, no matter how painful that truth is to speak or to hear. No matter how many people want to keep the "family secret" under wraps, the secret is a real person with real emotions which are being manipulated in the name of silence. Whether they are in on the "secret" and told to pretend that Granny is Mama, or kept in the dark and possibly the only member of the family who doesn't know – the truth has a way of surfacing – and the longer it stays buried, the more damage it will do when it comes out.

Children need to know their story, to know their place in the family. Allowing your grandson to believe he is your son, or your niece to believe she is your daughter, only to have them learn otherwise on their own at a later age, is not only cruel and painful, it is dishonest. Children look to their caregivers and other adults for honesty and guidance. A betrayal of this magnitude can have devastating, even lifelong consequences as the child discovers that people cannot be trusted – and that they themselves are not who they always believed themselves to be.

I can still remember the sense of something breaking apart deep inside me the day I discovered that my adopters were in fact my aunt and uncle. At twelve years old I couldn't put words to my thoughts or emotions, but it was incredibly demeaning to find out they hadn't trusted me with the truth all that time. My aunt preferred to play mother to me than assume her rightful role as my aunt.

Not only did that diminish my mother's own place, it robbed me of the aunt I should have had as well. My mother was an only child, and my father had two sisters, one of whom died at 17. I had no cousins at all, no extended family in the country I grew up in, no grandparents close by, no contact with my mother or anyone on her side of the family.

It was as if she ceased to exist the day she – reluctantly – signed me over to my aunt and uncle.

I grew up with divided loyalties. I loved my dad and wanted more contact with him, but my aunt refused to acknowledge him as my father, and expressed her regret in "letting" me meet him because she felt I cast my uncle aside. The truth is, I always had a hard time accepting my uncle, because I'd already spent nearly two years in England with my real daddy. If only she had given me the freedom to accept her husband as my uncle, herself as my aunt, and my dad as my father. In attempting to force my love and loyalty, she ultimately lost both.

The stereotypical adoption narrative portrays the adopting couple as older than average parents, fairly well-off – since they both work, and have no children to provide for – and for any number of reasons, unable to conceive or to carry a baby full-term. They spend years preparing to adopt, waiting for a baby, decorating a nursery, choosing clothes and names, making decisions based on their future as adoptive parents. A house with a yard, close to schools, in a neighborhood filled with kids.

In an emergency relative adoption, such as mine was made out to be, none of this exists. My aunt and uncle were certainly older than average, old enough to be grandparents. They had no solid, long-term marriage plagued by fertility issues. Still practically newlyweds, neither one with a college education, both immigrants in the country they brought me to, they had no children of their own – a matter of choice rather than capability, as I always believed.

My aunt's husband was not expecting her to bring me over from England. Little did he know that he'd have to put up with me under his roof for the next sixteen years, or what a strain that would be on all three of us. During those early months there was no house or yard, just an adults-only apartment complex, which served them an eviction notice because I violated their tenant agreement.

My aunt had already taken time off work for her father's funeral, so when she brought me and my grandmother home with her and my grandmother eventually left, she put me in full-time daycare. Within a year of my arrival in this strange new land, I'd been subjected to two more moves, one being an interim stay with a bachelor friend of my aunt's while they searched for a house. I also got moved to a different daycare.

So many changes in surroundings and caregivers, combined with the loss of both parents and grandparents, proved too much for me to handle and I became withdrawn, antisocial, and shut down, retreating into a fantasy world more often than not.

I strongly believe that potential adoptive parents need counseling prior to the adoption, counseling which includes coming to terms with any fertility problems and related feelings of inadequacy, grieving biological children lost to miscarriage or death, examining their desire to adopt and the reasons behind it, and most importantly, understanding the trauma, loss, and upheaval their future adopted child has already suffered and will continue to suffer with the added burden of adapting to a new family, perhaps in a new country.

When my mother took me to live with my grandparents at about six months of age, fleeing my father's abuse and violent temper, they were familiar to me. They'd been part of my life from the beginning, as much as I know. I have little knowledge and no memory of the year I spent with them, of how I handled my mother's leaving me in their care during an extended visit with her own parents, or how they handled me in her absence. I probably showed signs of grief and trauma, which they, lacking any psychological background, fumbled their way through. I probably suffered some attachment issues. I may have resisted my grandmother's attempts to care for me in my mother's place. But I knew them.

When my aunt swooped in and took over my care, I did not know her. My grandfather had just died, my father was in jail (which nobody told me, but it explains why he didn't prevent her from taking me), and suddenly here was this stranger trying to step in and replace the mother I'd lost. A mother who, I have very recently learned, was never notified of my grandfather's death or given the opportunity to come back for me.

My aunt and grandmother conspired to remove me from the country without her knowledge. I now lived with two strangers who, despite being relatives, were previously unknown to me. They did not share my history as my grandparents had. From my perspective, it was no different from the child in a foreign orphanage handed over to two strangers and never seeing home again. Abduction, with paperwork to make it legal.

Still they should have gotten some counseling in order to ease the transition for everyone involved. With all the adjustments they suddenly had to make, it never occurred to them that I might have trouble adjusting myself, especially to several new caregivers – including the daycare people. Above all, they should have been honest with me right from the start about who they were to me, and provided some form of continuity between my early life and the one they pushed me into.

In her book "Toddler Adoption: The Weaver's Craft" (Perspectives Press, 1997) Mary Hopkins-Best writes: "Ignoring feelings of anger or grief is confusing to a toddler at a time in her cognitive development when 'magical thinking' is common. When parents pretend that their toddler's former caregivers don't exist, her magical thinking might lead her to a number of erroneous conclusions. She might decide that they didn't really exist, that a former caregiver has simply disappeared, or that she lived in some fantasy place to which she might return as quickly as she left."

This "magical thinking" ran wild during my childhood. By avoiding my questions about my parents, my adopting aunt and uncle provided the ideal breeding ground for a wide range of imagined scenarios. Apparently, the imaginative toddler or preschool child is impressionable enough to be easily "gas lighted," or prone to cognitive or sensory manipulation by primary caregivers. Rather than allowing me the secure, logical awareness that they were my aunt and uncle and I'd been cared for by my parents and grandparents – who did not magically disappear – their insistence on secrecy eventually resulted in my populating the Kingdom of Magical Thinking with vague, nameless shadow people who might someday come back for me. That would explain my shock at discovering I'd been with blood relatives all along.

If the post-adoption therapist I am becoming could speak to my aunt and uncle nearly four decades ago, I would tell them to ask my mother's permission to take me into their temporary care, and leave me in my own home until she gave her consent. If they absolutely had to take me for a while, their role must be as guardians or caregivers, with no adoption involved. They could have raised me as their niece and allowed me to keep the name I was born with.

There was no excuse not to tell me whose child I am, whose grandchild I am. They should have put a photo album together for me, with my parents and grandparents and all of the information that other kids take for granted. I don't know my birth weight or length. I don't know the name of the doctor who delivered me or the nurse who assisted. I had to write the hospital and find out the time of day I was born and make sure of my birth date, because if a birth certificate can be amended, how much information can they change? I have three baby photos – prior to leaving England – in my possession, two of which I obtained from my father's collection after his passing.

To this day I'm fascinated by other people's baby photos, genetic history, family pictures, tracing the similarity of parents, children, siblings, nieces, nephews, grandchildren. Their unbroken family lineage. Every one of them has something I don't. Even somebody adopted as a newborn has something I don't, an unbroken story after the original separation from their natural mother. It's as if I ceased to exist at the age of 21 months and some other being took over. I lost my place in the family. I lost myself.

Survival Tips for the Adoptee:

Being adopted "in family" carries the same original relinquishment trauma as being adopted by strangers; it does not diminish or erase the "primal wound". You were separated from your natural mother. Even if you grew up with her as your "big sister" or "favorite aunt", you missed out on being mothered by the woman who gave birth to you. You need the same healing as any other adoptee. Do not allow anyone to deny you this.

Relative adoptions increase the possibility of a "family conspiracy". Everyone else knows that you were a product of your "sister's" teenage rebellion, or your "aunt's" extramarital affair while your "uncle" was stationed overseas, or your "cousin" had a problem with drugs and couldn't keep you. You've suspected they were hiding some vital information from you, but growing up resembling at least one side of your family, you didn't really suspect you were adopted.

You may be a Late Discovery Adoptee. Again, being "kept in the family" doesn't diminish your wounds, your pain. You've been betrayed by the people closest to you, and you don't have the luxury of seeking out your biological family in the hopes of belonging there. You're already with them. Maybe you see them all the time at family get-togethers or reunions.

You have the right to your feelings of betrayal and anger, and the right to assemble your own identity separate from your family, adopted and/or biological.

You have the right to choose who you call your parents. Maybe your natural mother feels more like the older sister or cousin you've always been told she was. Or maybe referring to your grandparents as "parents" feels as if you're living a lie. Maybe you believe your adopting aunt lost the right to be called "Mom" when you learned she held you beyond the reach of your natural parents for so many years. Call them whatever you feel most comfortable with. Relatives should be able to do a family guardianship without shame or secrecy, without altering your birth certificate or changing your name.

You have the right to grieve. You have suffered loss. Like any other adoption, relative adoptions can take place for a number of reasons. Maybe you remember living with your natural parents; maybe the family members who took you in allowed you the gift of time and space to grieve. Remember that grief has no timeline, and triggers are everywhere. You can be "fine" for a long time, until a trigger hits you from out of nowhere. Let yourself grieve. It's good to have a safe person in your family, someone who remembers your parents if they are deceased, to talk with when you're feeling this way.

Above all, remember that you are a separate entity. You are your own person. Relinquishment and adoption are significant and traumatic events, but they do not have the exclusive power to define you.

Survival Tips for Relatives Adopting:

If adopting an "illegitimate" baby from another family member, be honest from the beginning. The shame surrounding out-of-wedlock births is far less than what it used to be. It is not beyond a young child's understanding that he or she is being raised by grandparents, aunts or uncles, or cousins in place of the parents.

Follow the child's lead when it comes to establishing what to call whom; don't make demands, and allow changes to come as the child matures. If she turns ten and decides to start calling you Grandma instead of Mama, for example, don't assume she's doing it as an act of rebellion or distancing herself. Her thought processes are changing, and chances are she still loves you just as much; she feels more comfortable defining your relationship in these terms.

Understand that keeping a child within the biological family, or at least one side of it, does not minimize the trauma of loss or its effects. The more open you are to walking this journey with the child and understanding the impact of loss on his or her life, the stronger your relationship will become. Betraying his or her trust during a vulnerable time will weaken the relationship and threaten the trust he or she might place in others as time goes by. After all, you're not only raising a child, you are influencing an adult and shaping the parent he or she may become someday. Encourage honest communication, even when it's painful for both of you.

If raising a child in close proximity to one or both natural parents, please make sure the parents are aware that honesty is the best policy and will remain so. The child will not be lied to, told half-truths (use discretion and age-appropriate information, but children do understand more than most adults give them credit for) or have their fragile trust shattered. Mainly, the child needs reassurance that his or her needs take precedence over others' desire for secrecy. The child's needs also take precedence over the adoptive or guardian relative's desire for a child of her own. If you are the grandmother or aunt, especially if the child already knows you as such, do not ask or expect to be called "Mom". Not only is this hurtful and damaging to the child, it is also disrespectful to the natural mother, and may be perceived as a slap in the face, particularly if there is ongoing contact.

Divided loyalties are a normal consequence of adoption, as they are of divorce, and the child is going to share many of the same emotional and mental conflicts with children of divorce. These must be handled with the same sensitivity and not assumed they will "go away" over time as the child "gets used" to the adoption. If the natural parents choose to distance themselves from the child, that is up to them, but you need to make it clear to the child that he or she is not the cause of this distancing and must not blame herself for it. Just as children of divorce will guilt themselves over the family breakdown and any consequent relocation on the part of either parent, so will the child of open and/or relative adoption.

Above all, relative adoption must be kept open. The secrecy inherent in closed adoption is detrimental enough to an adoptee's mental health and capacity for trust. In a relative adoption, keeping it "closed" results in a conspiracy that everyone but the adoptee participates in. When the truth finally comes to light, as truth has a way of doing, the consequences are even more devastating. "You knew all along, and didn't tell me!"

When the entire family stands against the closed door, locking up the truth, the entire family is seen as traitorous when the lock breaks and the truth escapes.

One of the most tragic things about my own adoption story is that I was led to believe, from the beginning, that my mother did not want me. Between the ages of two and twelve, I was never told one thing about her, including her identity. My aunt preferred to maintain the fairy tale that she was the only mother who wanted me, as if she could obtain my love and loyalty by default.

The discovery that my mother never intended to give me up, nor willingly did so, shattered me. I feel as if my aunt cheated me out of my parents, and them out of me. She robbed me of the life I should have had. My grandmother should have insisted on my being told the whole truth while she was alive; our relationship might have been different.

If the natural parents are still living, and the child is relinquished rather than orphaned, the entire family must decide whether adoption truly is in the child's best interest, or if some form of family foster arrangements would serve them better. Circumstances can and do change. The day may come when the natural mother and/or father can provide a safe, nurturing, loving home for their own child. One of the arguments against open adoption is that the child may fear being taken back by the natural mother, or returned to her. Don't presume to know the child's thoughts or feelings on this subject. She may want to be returned to her mother. Let her know she can speak freely without shame or fear of condemnation, and that you won't make her feel guilty for wanting the natural mother-child bond strengthened or restored.

Like anyone else, adopted children need to know the safety of being listened to, valued, loved, cared for, and respected. This includes allowing their voice in the decision-making process regarding boundaries, visits, names, and their rightful place in the family.

Jodi Haywood – born in England and taken to North America two years later by an aunt she'd never met, Jodi grew up in a closed relative adoption and began writing stories at an early age to make up for the story nobody wanted to tell her – her own.

She pursued a degree in creative writing in college and is currently studying adoption-related issues such as developmental trauma and attachment disabilities.

She contributed to the anthology *Adoption Therapy: Perspectives from Clients and Clinicians on Processing and Healing Post-Adoption Issues* (Entourage, 2014) and has authored two young adult novels and the memoir *Attachment Unavailable* (to be released in 2015). When she isn't writing, she enjoys spending time with her husband and daughter, traveling around the U.S., and running marathons.

Letters to My Adoptive Mom*

by Lynn Steinberg

Back in 2009, my therapist at the time asked me to write a series of letters. The assignment was to write letters I would have wanted my adoptive mother to write to me as a young girl. The task challenged my loyalties to my mother and made me feel very icky and uneasy. However, the healing that took place as a result was remarkable. As I read the letters aloud in the therapist's office, I cried and cried like a lunatic. If only my mother had known what to say or do when it came to adoption. If only she had the tools. The truth is she had nothing. She was handed a baby and was told that it was her own. In her mind, I was a blank canvas.

I have not looked at these entries since writing them five years ago. It took my breath away as I read through them earlier this morning. The way in which I wished my mother had spoken to me is a mirror of the way I am parenting my adopted daughter. These letters no longer evoke any huge emotions in me. I still wish my mother voiced these things to me to make my journey to self easier, but I am getting there on my own and that is incredibly empowering. She is by my side now [every day for five years] and we are walking together through my healing now. It's important to note that these letters were never sent to my mother, nor were they meant to be. She will be reading them for the first time now along with all of you.

Dear Lynnie Bin (my mother's nickname for me),

I want you to know that it is okay to love your birth mom. It is okay if you even refer to her as mom. She is your mom as am I. You have two moms and that is okay. That is what makes you special. Being adopted is very painful. It is okay if you ever want to talk about your mom or ask me questions about adoption. I will try my best to answer them and if I cannot I will find someone that can. It is so hard to lose someone you love. Just because you don't know your birth mom does not mean you can't love her. It is okay to love her. It is okay if you even love her as much as me or even if you love her more than me. I think you should have a heart for your birth mom and a heart for me. Know that it is okay - you can keep these two hearts separate.

The truth is that I do not know why you were put up for adoption. When you grow up, perhaps we can find out what your story is. I am sorry that we do not have too much information, but I do not mind telling you the information we do have over and over again. Everyone has a story. Yours may be short and incomplete, but you do have a story.

Love, Mom

Dear Lynn,

I am so sorry that those girls in class whispered about you being adopted. I will call their mothers and explain to them more about adoption. People whisper and stare at people when they do not know about it. Just because they are whispering does not mean something is wrong with you. It just means they don't understand. I can also give your teacher some books about adoption or I can come to your class and we can teach your friends more about adoption. Whatever the best thing is for you, I will do. If you don't want me to do anything, just know that I would do anything if you asked me to.

Love, Mom

Dear Lynn,

I am so sorry I cried all those times you were mad and said I was not your real mom. I know that was a cry for help and I turned the other cheek - I made it about me. I always made you feel guilty for saying those words, instead I owe you an apology. When our fights settled down, I should have spoken to you more about your feelings. We all want our moms when we are mad or frustrated. These are confusing times for you. Although it is not okay to hurt people deliberately, I realize that those words, in particular, are your way of expressing how much you miss your mom. You needed to deal with the pain and anger of losing her. Because I never helped you do that, all your pain and anger is being brought into everyday situations. I am sorry I never helped you separate the pain, fear and loss of your mother with the trials of everyday life. Please forgive me.

Love, Mom

Have any of you used this letter writing method to help heal from your adoption loss? Did you find it effective? Do you feel I am being disloyal to my mother by publishing these very personal thoughts? I look forward to hearing from you.

Lesson learned: When you decide it's time to begin to heal from the trauma of adoption, let down the guard that adoptees often put up to protect the feelings of our adoptive parents. Be vulnerable and don't feel guilty finally voicing the emotions you repressed for so long. The adoption was not your choice and you have the right to feel the way you want to.

*originally published at Lost Daughters August 25, 2014

Lynn Steinberg is an adult adoptee from Chapel Hill, North Carolina. Her adoption was closed and Lynn's adoptive parents knew nothing about her birth family or story leading up to her relinquishment. At the age of 35, after having two biological children, Lynn and her husband Michael adopted a baby girl from Ethiopia. It was the adoption of her daughter that ignited an innate interest in searching for her birth mother.

In 2009, Lynn found her birth mother and half-siblings with the help of a private investigator. Upon reunion, she discovered that her existence had been kept a secret from her siblings by her birth mother for 35 years. With that said, Lynn was joyously accepted by her birth mother and siblings, but continually struggles with her identity and comfort level within her birth family. She feels there is a lack of support and resources for adult adoptees once the initial reunion is complete and hopes to act as a source of support for what she calls, "the reunion after the reunion."

Lynn is a strong advocate for opening adoption records nationwide and is passionate about educating adoptive parents on the importance of open communication and lifelong emotional support of their adopted children.

Lynn also writes for Lost Daughters and works for Roots Ethiopia, a non-profit organization that focuses on supporting community identified solutions for education and job creation in Southern Ethiopia.

PART III: SURVIVING SEARCH AND REUNION

The Road to My Truth

by Kara Albano

People have the right to know who they are. As Mark Twain once said, "The two most important days in your life are the day you are born and the day you find out why". I have done years of advocating, speaking privately to friends and family, and going to public rallies, writing letters, and shouting from the rooftops. I believe the right to know is personal, and varies from person to person, but I've always thought that, for me at least, that it was about choice. It's the right to know, not necessarily the right to search, harass, or do harm, but the right of choice.

If you do decide to search, do it respectfully. This is the woman or man who started you from a seed. Respect them as the ones who gave you life. And if you do make contact, and it doesn't go so well, please remember that you have made a choice– it's yours– own it. You made the choice to search or to hold off, to find, to approach (however you saw fit), you made the choice to let people into your life, and you made the choice to kick them out if they weren't to your liking. As an infant or young child we lost that choice, but by deciding to search, we took back that choice, and said, "This is my life, this is my history, my future and finally my choice."

I was lucky enough to be a part of a small, but wonderful group of people here in Rhode Island (where I was born and raised) who advocated for adoptee rights and freedom called RICARE. We wrote letters, made phone calls, participated in small rallies, and I'm sure, bugged the heck out of many people. This went on for many years, and for many years we held on to some glimmer of hope, any chance, that one day we could make a difference.

We sat in on numerous statehouse meetings and spoke out about the injustice of sealed original birth certificates of adoptees. I remember one statehouse meeting, my first, I believe, I was close to the last to read my speech. Everyone before me talked about the facts, the statistics of good reunion, medical history and such. I had chosen to go the emotional route, to be fair, I thought that was what everyone was doing.

We had all written our speeches the night before. So here I was, miss "live behind my mask," miss "never let them see your emotions" pouring my heart (and childhood fears and insecurities) out to a room full of strangers, and some of the most important people in the state.

I almost died. I was shaking so badly, and literally sweating buckets. I was soaked towards the end, but I did it. My (adoptive) mother (my biggest supporter through all of this) who had never been silent a day in her life, attended and sat quietly to the side, even though I know she had a ton to say.

As the room was packing up to leave, my mother turned to me and whispered "hold my purse," which I guess was equal to a woman taking off her earrings before a fight. My mother then stood up, held her head high, and politely tore through every single point our opponents brought up that day. I listened, overjoyed that for once she wasn't arguing against me. I knew how being on the losing end of her lectures felt.

After many statehouse meetings, whether it was my over emotional story, my mother's spit fire ways, or my friend bringing in her children (proving that medical history affects all), it worked. The day the open records law passed, was also the day the Boston Bruins won the Stanley Cup, another huge victory for a small region. Two glorious victories in the same day, and my brain filed it as "the law and the cup". (It was far too emotional to remember any detail). I do, however, remember that after the vote was in, our group yelled so loudly that we were asked by statehouse officials to keep quiet in the halls. This prompted another lecture from my mother, once again not aimed at me. ("Don't you realize what just happened here? How long people waited for this?").

On July 2, 2012, I received my original birth certificate, and you couldn't put a word on my emotions. The whole way through the line, while I was getting handed my paper, and the days after it, were one big blur. I started thinking about that little paper I was holding and all the information that it contains. I had never had my name, and a name is an identity, something that makes you, you. A name is what we came into the world as; it is overwhelmingly significant, and equally as powerful. A name is a nationality that we are a part of, a history that we don't know that we made, a life that we never knew we had.

Not only does our name hold such a power, but a few other names hold that power as well. We not only have a name, but we have one other crucial part to us, we have a woman's name as well (and possibly a man's name). A stranger who holds the key to all the information we need to possess. I must have looked at that piece of paper for hours every day, holding it up like it was some sort of reward for the world to see. This is proof in writing that I exist. Proof that my struggles have been rewarded, and for once I was able to look at the moment my life began. Though my birth name is not on my birth certificate, the fact that I have a mother's name is proof that I was born. How many people had to wait until they were 29 to prove they were born?

How can one name – just one name – that I've discovered is extremely common, be so powerful for two women, my birth mother and I? Her name can break me down into a million pieces, and at the same time lift me up to the highest mountain peak. It can bring me to tears, or put a huge smile on my face, and make me giddy. There is so much hiding behind a name: medical history, family trees, historical stories, laughter, memories, and photographs. They are all people with names, people with stories, and they are my biological family.

I did eventually search and find, and I can tell you the ups and downs of every emotion I felt, and still feel to this day. How I would randomly burst into tears, in very awkward places in the weeks following my first email correspondence with my biological mother, the long nights without sleep, and the first time I met my new brothers, my cousins, my aunts and uncles, my mother's husband, and my grandparents. I could tell you about every tear I cried from joy, and the ones from pain.

I have learned the level of impact my relinquishment brought to my biological family. I never knew the pain cut through my maternal family as deeply as it has. I always thought that the loss was mother, father, child not mother, father, child, grandparent, sibling, aunts, uncles, cousins, and I can spread that out even wider. I'm not going to lie, it hits me like a ton of bricks to this day. Each family member had a story of what they remembered, what they had been told, how it felt to lose me, and then getting me back.

I have learned that true love reaches through the ages, and missed birthdays, through vacant memories that shadow what could have been. Love can shine through it all, in a way that makes the whole reunion feel so surreal and dreamlike. The best advice I can give you here is to strap in and hold on tight, and prepare for a wild ride.

I have also learned of more than my share of disappointments. Please remember, not everyone is open and understanding. Now is the time to make a choice and say to yourself, as I have many times, "I now have the choice to keep you in my life, or cut you out. I am an adult, no longer a baby, and I have the power of making my own decisions!" Trust me, making that choice, holding that power that you never had before, lessens the impact. It's empowering. It may sound corny but it's true. Try it. Another line of mine is "Hey I've survived (insert number of years here) without you, will not knowing you change me in anyway?" The answer is no. Reunion can only add, it can't take away what was never there to begin with.

I learned that my non-identifying information from the orphanage was mostly lies, and the story that my mother named me Cheryl Ann after her social worker, and the nurse who delivered me, was false. I think that hit me the hardest. I had gone through life thinking that they treated my mother so well, that she wanted to pass on the two names, or as my adoptive mother always thought, she wanted to leave a trail of bread crumbs to help me find her. Neither was true – my mother never named me. She wanted my name to be something special between my adoptive parents and I.

The best advice I can give to others is, yes it hurts to be told lies, and to have believed them your whole life, but to keep moving on. Realize there is so much more to discover than little details, and you will hopefully have many years to correct the falsehoods, or educated guesses. And guess what? Eventually you cry or scream it all out, and you pick up the pieces, as you have done your whole life, and move on. In the grand scheme of things you have the truth now, and next to that, the lies seem so little.

Many people ask me my opinion on adoption, like I'm some expert because I lived it. For some reason every person has the same question, "Do you like being adopted?," "How does it feel?," or "Do you wish you weren't adopted?"

That's a long answer with a lot of contradictions, and typically I don't go into it. I have my own thoughts and feelings, but one thing I do always say is, "how can I hate something that is so much a part of me?"

It's my history, as much a part of me as my brown eyes. It's nothing more than a fact on a paper, with emotions behind it. I firmly believe everyone is meant to walk the path they are on. It has shaped me. I've met and become friends with people I would never have known, if I didn't live the life I had. I have memories, good and bad, which made me grow. What if I was never relinquished, would my half siblings not exist? If that were the case, I would miss out on wonderful relationships with them.

Back to that question on whether or not I like being adopted, or wish I wasn't adopted. I always answer that question by saying "At my birth, five pebbles were handed out: one to my biological mother, one to my biological father, one to my adoptive mother, one to my adoptive father, and one for me. Each of us threw our pebbles into the water, at that time, and watched the ripple effect. The ripple from each pebble will determine where our life takes us from that one event."

Now that I am in reunion, I realize we need a lot more than five pebbles. One for each grandparent who lost a grandchild, one for an aunt or an uncle who lived with a pregnant sister who returned without a baby, one for each of my brothers who grew up thinking my mother had no other children, and one for my cousins. Hundreds of pebbles, given out to friends, family (both adopted and biological), teachers, and co-workers, everyone that I have come in contact with. All shaped by one act, a decision by two people to relinquish, and two people to adopt, a very long time ago. So, in the grand scheme of things, how can you hate or love something that has changed fate for so many? You can't. You just need to accept.

So take life for what it gave you, whether it makes you or breaks you, follow your own path. Everything that has happened to you is just a single piece of your life. Don't let people change who you are, or think less of you because you are adopted, or chose to search or not to search. Embrace yourself and always remember you matter.

Kara Albano was born in early November of 1982. She was relinquished at birth and spent the first seven months of her life in St. Vincent's home, an orphanage run by Catholic Social Services in Providence, RI. At seven months, she went to live with the family who would eventually adopt her close to her first birthday.

With the help of her adoptive mother, Jackie, Kara started searching for her biological family at the age of 13. She has been involved in many groups pertaining to adoptee rights. Kara was a member of RI-CARE (Rhode Island Coalition for Adoptee Rights and Equality) a local adoptee group in RI that fought to get laws overturned, in regards to sealed birth certificates. She is also an active member of RIARG (Rhode Island Adoptee Resource Group), as well as serving on the Board of Directors for the Adoptee Rights Coalition.

Due to the success of RI-CARE in the summer of 2011, almost 17 years after the start of her search, Kara was able to finally reunite with many biological family members. Kara also helped her adopted brother and his biological family reunite in 2013.

Even though Kara is in a successful reunion, she still fights for other states to promote equality for adoptees, and is a confidante for other adoptees in her life. Kara now works at a group home for teenage girls who are in state care for reasons such as psychiatric, behavioral, children looking for families, and also kids from juvenile courts.

How Do I Trust That I Won't Fail?

by Daryn Watson

"You miss 100% of the shots you don't take." – Wayne Gretzky

I was adopted at the age of seven months in the town of Peace River in northern Alberta, Canada. Both my parents worked and they had a daughter on their own, though it was a rough pregnancy. My parents picked me up at the Alberta government adoption agency in Edmonton, the capital of Alberta. I had primarily been in one foster care home until the weekend before I went home with my new family.

My shoes and clothes were too small and I had been neglected (not cleaned very well). My mom sent my dad to a department store next to the office building where the adoption offices were to get me some new clothes. She would later file a complaint with the Alberta government over my condition.

My parents, especially my dad, noticed I would begin crying every time he picked me up, seemingly for no reason. I would learn many years later, through hypnotherapy, that the man of the foster family I was placed with was abusive towards me. This created a fear I had of men, even my dad, throughout my life.

I've lived much of my life in self-doubt, afraid of trying new things, new jobs or careers because I am deeply afraid of failure. Constantly I go through my life with a desire to change things in my life such as losing weight or applying for jobs and allowing myself the opportunity to experience new opportunities.

Often times, I get excited thinking about starting a new career that is different from my landscape maintenance business I've had for the last 23 years. I've wanted to become a psychologist or therapist, a tennis coach, a banker, or something else that I think I would be satisfied with. I usually take a few steps researching some type of new career, but inevitably the excitement and drive fades away after a short time and I remain stuck with the same unfulfilling career I still have.

My career is secure at times and I know how to do the work, but my passion for landscaping is not there. There are aspects of my profession I still enjoy but I feel deftly unchallenged and unhappy much of the time.

Most times I felt a need for approval from my parents that I was making the right choice at something. If I didn't get the approval, I felt like I royally messed up. Much of my life I competed in sports and athletics and was quite good at many of them. Internally I felt if I was "good enough" in whatever sport I competed in (hockey, track and field, racquetball, baseball, and later in life, tennis) that my parents and others around me would find I was worth something and I would be accepted.

In 2009, I decided I wanted to be the top tennis player in Texas in my division. I made the decision to hire a personal trainer to improve my fitness and I took a lot of private lessons. After a month, I won my first major tournament. I would win a few more that season or at least make the finals. This enabled me to make the end of the year Master's tournament which included the top eight players in the state at each division.

The tournament consisted of two groups of four who played a round robin against each other. The top seed in each group would play in the final. My dad came to watch my third match, which was very competitive but I ended up losing. This placed me into a three-way tie for first and my dream of making the final was in jeopardy. Luckily, I was able to make the final based on percentage points.

However, inside I felt a sense of disappointment because I did not win in front of my dad. I knew he was proud of me and my effort during that match but deep down I felt a lot of criticism within myself for not sweeping all three matches in my pool.

The next day I played the final against an opponent who had beaten me twice earlier in the year. We had a young tennis referee for the final and I had a couple of disputed calls go my way. This infuriated my opponent early on and he began to imply that I was a cheater. In turn, I felt this was an injustice and I began to lose focus on my tennis game and I bought into his bullshit ego accusations.

We split the first two sets 6-1, 1-6. He won the first game of the third set and his ego was out of control, making the match very unpleasant. I told myself, "Maybe it's time to retire from this match and get away from his anger and negativity." I just didn't want to deal with his crap.

Then some thoughts entered my mind. "Breathe. Relax. Play your game and don't worry about him." I won the next game, the game after that and so on. I found myself up 5-1 with the serve. I went to the back fence to towel off, which was part of my ritual. I turned around and saw my opponent walking towards the bench.

"It's only 5-1" I said to him. "I know. I quit," he replied. I wasn't sure what to do or what happened but he left the court. As he walked up the stairs to the clubhouse, my wife heard him mutter "I don't lose to cheaters!"

Even though I had won the match and the tournament and I finished number one in my division for the year, I felt a huge letdown because of the circumstances. I felt my opponent took my joy away from what I had accomplished. The situation felt ugly to me and I began asking myself if I deserved to win or if others would feel the same way.

What bothered me even more was how my opponent had turned on me during the match. Both times when he had beaten me before, he was nice and even offered to play doubles with me at tournaments. But when the tables turned and I was the victor, his nastiness came out. I know this can happen in any sport with most people who lose (I'm not the most gracious loser in the world). For him to call out my character and integrity hurt very deeply inside. Sadly, to this day, my opponent and I do not speak to each other.

During this time of my quest to conquer the tennis world, my birth mother was giving me a lot of praise. Our relationship seemed okay to me (from what I could gather). Her youngest son was getting married that September and they were going to have a reception in southern Alberta. My wife and I were invited.

My brother did not attend my wedding a few years earlier. My birth mother told me he had "too many taxes to pay" to make the trip down. I felt disappointed but I let it go. I felt conflicted if we should attend his reception or not but ultimately I declined the invitation via email. I did not realize until weeks after the reception that I had mistakenly transposed the names on the email and I sent it to the wrong email address.

My birth mother sent me a very hurtful email, claiming I did not care about her son or family because I had not replied to the invitation properly. She said my brother had let it go but she would not let it go. I apologized for not sending the reply to the correct email address and I even forwarded a reply from the couple who received the erroneously sent emails. Yes there were three that I had sent to the wrong address by mistake.

My birth mother was so angry that she would not read the email proving my mistake. She even said "you can spend all your time flying around Texas going to tennis tournaments but you can't even bother to contact your brother about his wedding reception." Again I felt my character and integrity being questioned.

I asked her, "In your opinion, what would be the proper way to reply to the wedding invitation?" She replied, "By sending a card and a gift" (she is very big on cards).

So I sent my brother and his new bride a card along with a gift card and an apology. I informed my birth mother of my deed. Her reply was "well, don't send it on my accord."

"What the hell? Really lady?" First you chastise me for not properly replying to the invitation and then I make amends and it's still not satisfactory to you?

I had had enough of this crap. I told my birth mother on the phone, "You could have taken 10 seconds to write me an email to ask if we were coming to the reception or not. But no, instead you chose to be angry and create this drama and story about how I treated you and your son and family."

Her reply was that she was too busy with all the reception plans etc. It sounded like a lot of excuses to me (as usual). I was at my boiling point with her and I became very heated.

I told her that I was tired of receiving angry and nasty emails and letters from her and if this bullshit continued, this relationship would be over permanently! I could not believe I said that to her, but I had come to a point in our relationship where I didn't need her in my life. There is a huge difference to wanting a healthy relationship and feeling you need to hold onto something that is unhealthy.

That October I received a short email for our 14th reunion anniversary. She said she felt we could possibly build on something positive between us for the future. The message sounded encouraging.

However, the next month, while attending a local adoption conference, I received another email from her. It read:

"IT'S OVER!!!"

I began to cry almost immediately over this message. I made my way to the restroom and began crying almost uncontrollably. "Why would she write this?" I thought. We didn't have any communication between us and I didn't do anything to provoke her so what is with this message?

Thankfully I found an adoption counselor outside the restroom and I showed her the message. I had asked her a few months earlier if the relationship dynamic I had with my birth mother was "normal" and she said, "No, it wasn't normal or healthy."

She read the message and told me to "get angry (with her)." You don't need to be treated like this. I felt a little better but I was still stewing.

The next day, I arrived at a tennis league match quite early. I decided to reply to my birth mother. Now I know it is not wise to send messages when one is angry and charged and most of the time I try to follow this advice. But this time it was different for me. I thought "well if this is over between her and I, then I'm going down swinging!"

I typed on my IPhone 3 for at least fifteen minutes. I told her how hurt I felt by her words, her accusations, her lies, manipulations, excuses and bullshit. And then I told her to leave me and my wife and my family alone!

This wasn't the end of our barbs but my birth mother and I have come to some sort of truce after agreeing to not send each other anymore hurtful messages. This I can live with some sort of serenity by holding boundaries and knowing what my truth is.

We can't change other people and, through experience, I've learned that I've wasted a lot of time, energy and mileage on myself trying to please others and get their approval. We adoptees struggle with pleasing others but we can't please everyone.

We can learn to discover ourselves through writing in a journal, going to therapy and doing things and activities in our lives that bring us joy.

I'm grateful for finding my birth mother and having answers to my family and heritage. There comes a time when, I believe, we have to evolve from any relationship and ask ourselves "does this relationship serve me anymore? What am I gaining from staying in contact with this person? What is my payoff for having this person in my life?"

I'm learning to trust myself and slowly learning to cautiously trust others. If we don't take a calculated risk with others, then we likely won't live a very meaningful life.

Daryn Watson is a Canadian adoptee living in Austin, TX. Thanks to open records, he found his maternal birth family living in Canada in 1995 after a two month search. The reunion journey with his birth mother has been tumultuous at times but he is grateful for finding his birth mother and family.

Daryn reunited with a paternal brother (Aaron) in 2011 and remains in contact with him. His birth father has not made any effort to contact Daryn.

Daryn lives with his wife Christine and their several cats in Austin, TX. He works as a landscaper and a real estate investor. He enjoys racquet sports, reading, movies, meditating and writing about adoption issues.

On Life, Love and Survival of Your Adoption Reunion

by Nicole Blank

"The devil doesn't come dressed in a red cape and pointy horns.
He comes as everything you've ever wished for…" – Tucker Max

In the winter of 2011, the month I turned 40, I began the process of searching for my birth family. I'd never really seriously looked for them, but my adoptive mother had died suddenly from a surgical accident a year earlier and I felt maybe now was truly the time to get some answers. In many ways, I was lucky. I was adopted at 8 weeks of age and my birth surname had been left on my adoption documents by some miraculous accident, and I got an employee at the Pennsylvania adoption agency that still had my records from 1971 to 'slip' me my birth mother's first name.

I knew from my non-identifying information my birth mother's age and now I had her full name, and I also knew from the non-identifying information that I had a full sibling, a brother, who was a year older than me. By August of that same year, I'd found both my birth mother and my brother and I thought the long journey was finally over. In many ways, though, it had just begun.

Like many, if not all adoptees, I had a fantasy about who my birth family might be. What they might look like, where they'd work, whether I shared any personality traits with them. I would even look at strangers with similar features to me and wonder, "Is that one of them?" Would I know a family member if I saw him or her face to face?

I went as far as to only date men who looked completely dissimilar to me just in case a family member was lurking out there somewhere. Ironically, my heart knew more about my birth family than I was ever led to believe. The adoption agency in its infinite wisdom told my adoptive family that I was the first child of two teenagers – knowing full well I had three older siblings and my birth parents were 25 and 29, respectively.

I remember, more than once, telling my mother I truly felt like I had older brothers and she told me that was impossible. When in reality, I did have older brothers – two of them – and both men shared similar features to the constant image of an older brother I'd carried in my mind for as long as I could remember.

It took another month before I worked up the nerve to contact the first members of my birth family, but after that, my reunion moved alarmingly fast. I talked to my brother on the phone for the first time ever in September of 2011 and within two months we'd have a meeting and spend five full days getting to know each other. I'd find out from him that my birth mother had multiple sclerosis and at the age of only 65 had to be put in a nursing home.

In March of 2012, I met her for the first and only time in my life. She told me the name of my birth father and by May I'd found him and met him twice that year. I also made contact with my sister who shared my mother and my brother who shared my father. Not to mention many aunts, uncles, cousins, nieces and nephews. As wonderful as all of this sounds – and at the time to me it truly was an unimaginable high – I didn't see the crash coming on the other side of that high.

By the fall of 2012, I'd lost complete contact with my brother – by his choosing, not mine – who I honestly thought I had a lasting connection with. I'd only spent four hours with my other brother – all in one day – and I still hadn't met my sister. My birth father also decided he did not want any contact with me again and I was never to see or hear from my birth mother again either as she died that year from multiple sclerosis complications. I was completely unprepared for the fall. In many ways, I will never be the same person I was before I found and met my family. There is not much of a greater pain than being rejected or unwanted a second time.

And yet I ask myself this question daily – especially during down times – if I had to search for my family all over again, knowing what I know now, would I? And the answer still – despite the pain – is a resounding YES. Because looking back on it three years later I can say – there have been hidden blessings. I know who I look like. I know where my giddy laugh comes from, my sense of humor, my bad allergies and asthma, my lack of height. I know why I lean a certain way politically and I know why I hate dresses and heels and doing anything with my hair. I finally had a family tree. And I finally had proof that I came into the world like everyone else did and for reasons no less desirable than any other human being.

To be fair, my reunion was not a complete disaster. I still talk to my one brother – even if it's not as often I'd like to or how I'd pictured it – and I still hope to one day meet up with my sister. I have met my niece and nephew many times – the children of the brother who no longer talks to me – and have a great friendship with his ex-wife as well as with her family who accepted me with no holds barred. And my birth father's aunt and uncle – my great-aunt and great-uncle – and their extended family have also accepted me with love and without question despite my father walking away from me two years ago.

And I now even have a wonderful new friendship and email weekly with my paternal half-brother's mother who was married to my birth father years before I was conceived. I often think, "What could have been?" I need to continue to concentrate on what is right now and not press the future.

My reunion is nowhere near what the television, news reports, and online stories had me believing I would have. My one true mistake was going into my search hoping for the fairy tale. It is true – some lucky souls do receive the gift of an easy reunion – but for the rest of us, it's about finding the love that is out there for us to receive.

With each reunion, we as adoptees are literally entering the lives of complete strangers – regardless of how much blood and DNA we share with them – and asking them to fall in love with us from the start. Love doesn't work that way in any relationship. It takes time to grow. It has fits and starts. And sometimes, for even unknown reasons, love dies without us really knowing why. And it's how you deal with that last fact that determines how years from now, you'll view your adoption reunion. Entering any relationship expecting the other person to automatically love you is the surest way to be disappointed, and relatives are no exception to this rule.

I have survived my reunion and continue not only to survive, but to persevere and look forward to whatever future the world holds for me and the family who has chosen to stay with me. There are still many hard and painful days to be sure – but I wouldn't change a single action on my part or do one thing differently. I have found peace, ironically, in having less control of my life than I ever had before.

"God grant me the serenity to accept the things
I cannot change, the courage to change the things I can,
and the wisdom to know the difference."

In the spring of 1971, I was born as Lisa in Hanover, Pennsylvania to a 25-year-old woman and a 29-year-old man. I was the third child on both sides with two half-siblings and one full sibling, and was the only child out of my siblings given up for adoption. Two months later – after a stint in foster care –I was adopted and raised an only child outside of Baltimore, Maryland where I lived and went to college, only moving back to Pennsylvania at the age of 24 where I married in 1996 and had two children, brothers, two years apart.

Though I received a B.A. in psychology, I became a stay-at-home mother for many years until starting work part-time as a teller in a credit union. My hobbies - outside of writing - include advocating proper care for pet hermit crabs, psychic ability development, and ghost hunting as part of a local paranormal team. Interestingly, my ghost hunting has brought me back many times to Gettysburg, PA which is only mere miles from where my life began nearly 45 years ago. In so many ways, I have come full circle. – **Nicole Blank**

Five Survival Tips for Adoption Reunion

by Rebecca Hawkes

Find appropriate outlets for your "adoption crazy."

Adoption reunions can bring out the nutty in the best of us. Adoptees and first parents may both enter the reunion process with wounds and scars created by their separation from each other. Reunion also frequently triggers regression to an earlier age; the adoptee may regress to the emotional age of a young child and biological parents may find themselves traumatically "stuck" at the age of relinquishment in some aspects of their development. We may understand certain things with our logical brains while simultaneously experiencing strong emotions that defy and overpower logic.

Anger, jealousy, and fears of abandonment or rejection are all normal parts of the reunion experience. Our emotions are real and valid and often very insistent, but that doesn't mean we have to act on all of them. Take some time to let your emotions settle down before you send that email or text or post that Facebook status. Write the letter you never send. Paint a picture. Go for a walk. Call a trusted friend and rant to him or her. Find some strategy – whatever works for you – that will allow you to create some space before you say something you will regret to the person with whom you are creating a tender new relationship.

This isn't to say that you should never speak your mind. There may come a time in the reunion process when an open, honest expression of the hard stuff is exactly what is required to move the relationship forward. But proceed with care. Hurt people often do hurtful things, and the results can be devastating.

Find a network of supporters who truly understand what you are going through.

Adoption reunion is intense. It can bowl us over in unexpected ways, and often the people close to us don't know what to make of what is happening. Your spouse may not understand what you are experiencing. Your kids may not understand. Your best friend may not understand. The adoptive family probably won't understand. But there are people out there who will understand and be able to provide the support you need.

Through blogging, Facebook, and Twitter, I have been able to form a strong network of adoptee friends, and I cannot say enough about how important this network has become to me. Formerly, I was like one wandering alone in the wilderness. I had to try to make sense of all of my adoptive and reunion experiences on my own. Now I have companions, and they just get it.

Seek out an adoption-competent therapist.

This one certainly falls into the easier-said-than-done category, but it's not impossible. Therapists typically receive little training in adoption-specific issues, and they may even have been influenced by broad cultural beliefs about adoption that are less than helpful. But with a little effort, you may be able to find a therapist who is the right match for you and your reunion situation. Not every adoptee or first parent will find therapy necessary or helpful, but some may find that reunion stirs up issues that are best handled with the help of a professional. I recommend coming up with a list of questions to ask before you commit to working with any one person on a regular basis. Many therapists will also allow you to participate in a trial session before committing to more.

Remember that reunion is a process, not a destination.

It would be nice if reunion "fixed" everything, but it doesn't. In fact, it can open new wounds as we acquire new understandings of what was lost. Neither the adoptee nor the first parent is the person they would have been if the separation had never happened. We will have a different relationship in reunion than we would have had if we had stayed together. We need to allow ourselves space to mourn what was lost, while simultaneously appreciating the present-day relationship for what it is. It also helps to recognize that reunions go through many stages. Like all true relationships, they are dynamic and ever evolving.

Set boundaries with care.

Boundaries are a tricky part of the reunion process. As healthy adults, we sometimes need to set boundaries in order to create safe spaces for ourselves, but in adoption reunion emotional regression and fears of rejection on the part of one or both parties can result in misinterpretation of boundaries. If another member of your reunion situation has gotten sucked into "adoption crazy," you may need to create some space for your own sanity.

You do not need to get sucked into another person's drama, and certainly no one should remain in a situation that is abusive or harmful. But try not to meet crazy with crazy, or to respond to lashing out by lashing back. This is easier said than done, of course! But if you can manage it, attempt to communicate your need for limits in kind ways. Try to make it clear that your boundaries are about your own needs, not a rejection of the other person.

Of course, reunion volatility being what it is, the other person may perceive your communication as a rejection anyway, but at least you will have done your part to try to keep things civil. Meet the other person with care and kindness, if you can, but don't forget to extend the same care and kindness to yourself. Remember the airlines' dictum about putting on your own oxygen mask first, before attempting to help others.

Rebecca Hawkes is an adoptee by way of Baby Scoop Era infant adoption and a parent by way of birth, adoption, and foster care. She blogs about adoption, family, and other matters at Sea Glass & Other Fragments and The Thriving Child. Her work has also appeared at Adoption Voices Magazine, BlogHer, the Huffington Post, and Brain, Child magazine, and in the anthologies *Lost Daughters: Writing Adoption From a Place of Empowerment and Peace*, *Adoption Reunion in the Social Media Age*, and *Adoption Therapy: Perspectives from Clients and Clinicians on Processing and Healing Post-Adoption Issues.* She lives in Western Massachusetts with her husband, her three daughters, and a dog named Buddy.

My Story

by Holly Watson

I am adopted. You wouldn't know it because I have never been one to announce out loud, "Hey, I am adopted!" But even at 46 years of age, deep down I have always wondered, "Who am I?"

My adoptive mother tells me that for the first month or so, nothing or no one could console me – all I did was cry. After a lot of research over the years, I have learned that crying was my way of grieving for the mother that I had "lost," the mother who didn't want me. From a young age, I was aware of the fact I was adopted. I cannot recall the first time when I was told, or actually when I understood what adopted meant. Many times, I remember we read the book, "The Family That Grew" that explains to children about adoption. Honestly, I think it was enough times that I memorized the words on each page.

Growing up I would lie in bed at night and wonder why my birth mother didn't want me. What did I do that was so bad? It's difficult to explain to non-adoptees when they act as though our feelings are no big deal. We are supposed to be grateful because many children have grown up with so much worse. Yes, that is true, but to not understand why I wasn't wanted by the woman who gave birth to me, hurts.

In June of 1986, my friend, Mary Beth, and I had made a deal – five years after our high school graduation she was going to help me search for my birth mother. However, two years after we graduated, Mary Beth was killed. For a long time, I just didn't think I could honestly do the search without my friend. Mary Beth was the one who understood how I felt more than anyone else. Besides, I didn't want to hurt my parents by searching for a woman who didn't want me in the first place.

I decided not to tell my adoptive parents that I had decided to search, nor did I tell many of my friends for that matter. I always felt loved by my adoptive family, but I also felt incomplete, and that somehow it was my fault that my birth mother gave me away.

When I finally decided to search, I wrote a letter to the judge in the county where I was born expressing my interest in searching for my birth mother. I explained that I had young children and no medical background. The judge immediately responded to my letter and told me that he would issue a court order, but wanted to make sure I really wanted to locate her. He asked me to wait two weeks to have time to think about it before I responded. After the time passed, the kind judge issued a court order to Family Services and Children's Aid Society to do the search.

Shortly after, I received a call from a clerk stating she had received the court order and that the fee would be $60.00 an hour for the search. My husband and I had no idea how we were going to come up with that kind of money, but we would find a way. The woman explained that I would be receiving an update from her in about 6 weeks. Imagine my surprise when, less than 24 hours later, she called me back. I was thrilled with her news! The woman had made contact with my birth mother. We agreed on a date for me to finally meet her.

Meeting my birth mother in a church parsonage, I had so many hopes and dreams for us reconnecting. I don't think anyone can truly be prepared for a reunion; it is definitely a roller coaster of emotions. One of the first things I asked her was if she thought about me on my birthday. Celebrating my birthday has always been and still is a sad day for me. My birth mother told me she couldn't remember the exact day of my birth, but that she did know it was at the beginning of October. I have to admit, after all those years of wondering, I was crushed to find out that she didn't even remember the exact date.

At our reunion, I learned about my conception. It came as a bit of a shock to discover that she had lived with my birth father and his wife along with their four children. Yes, you read that correctly! And well, here I am … need I say more? I know it's weird. Go ahead and say it.

When I was born, my birth mother was 33 and my birth father was 41. My birth mother also had another daughter whom she had also placed for adoption 10 years prior to me, as well as raising a son. Neither of my siblings knew that I even existed.

I remember that night after meeting my birth mother not being able to sleep. Finally, I met this woman I had only fantasized about in the past. To be honest, although I was shocked and disappointed at the same time, more than anything, I just wanted her to WANT me in her life.

We did talk on the telephone more than once, but it was always like pulling teeth trying to get answers from her. All I knew was that my biological father passed away from cancer in 1983. She never shared any medical background about herself or her family.

I remember more than anything the one time that I was introduced to my maternal grandmother and aunts; my maternal grandmother wouldn't give me the time of day. I was my birth mother's dirty little secret; she moved as far away from me as she could!

One of my mutual friends was the go-between for introducing me to my birth brother and his wife. When my birth mother caught wind that there were plans in the making for me to be able to meet her son, she called me and was quite upset. She wanted to know why I would tell anyone about us and now her secret was out. I told her I didn't realize I wasn't supposed to tell anyone.

At first, our reunion was awkward. My birth brother wanted to know what had changed; he had heard from our mutual friend that I was excited about the opportunity for us to meet. I told him I would have been too, if our mother had not been so against it. He answered, "She should have told me about you." My brother, his wife and I talked at a park until almost midnight. We agreed to get together again soon so that our kids could meet. Things were new and they were good. Our families did a lot of things together: dinner, hanging out, going for hikes, playing games, and getting to know one another.

It's not clear why our mother still felt the need to treat me as her dirty little secret. On one occasion, just after my brother's wife gave birth to their son, she introduced me to some of her co-workers as her son's babysitter. There always seemed to be some jealousy and animosity on her part when it came to a relationship between me and my brother. As quickly as our relationship started, it abruptly came to an end.

In 1999, my friend suggested and even helped me write an ad for our local newspaper. It said that I was searching for my birth sister. On the day the ad was to run, the phone began to ring off the hook. At first, part of me was scared to answer the phone, but finally, my husband picked it up. As it turned out, the phone calls were from my birth sister's husband. I was thrilled but at the same time scared of possibly being rejected.

I remember with fondness my new-found sister and I having a long wonderful talk on that special day. Apparently, our birth mother had contact with her, but she had not told either of us about the other. My birth sister (also adopted) was glad that I had taken the initiative to find her. We hit it off right from the start after having the opportunity to meet in person. That day we learned that both of our sons are left-handed – something neither one of us could figure out where it came from. My sister and I email, send Christmas cards along with kids' updates, and see each other as often as possible.

When my brother learned that I had connected with our sister that had been placed for adoption, he was furious and said that he didn't have any sisters. For years, I sent my brother and his wife Christmas cards with pictures of my kids, but never heard anything back from him. When we would see any of his family out in public, it would break my heart all over again to have them not even acknowledge me.

A few years ago, my birth sister stopped to visit with me after she had been to see our birth mother. My birth sister said our mother had apologized for me finding her. Coming to my defense, my birth sister said that she should have just told her, instead of having to find out in some newspaper ad. Our birth mother went on to say that she would like to talk with me if I wanted to meet for coffee. In relaying this message, my birth sister suggested that I call her, but I opted to send a note instead. I had a small glimmer of hope for reconciliation. No response.

The next year I tried sending a similar note at the insistence of my birth sister. Again nothing. I shared pictures of my precious princesses; I wanted my birth mother to see what she was missing. In 2012, I decided to try one more time. I didn't want to call and put her in an awkward position. This time I did receive a response. My birth mother – the person I had only wanted to WANT me in her life – left such a disappointing message.

I finally made the decision that I must stop trying to reconcile after trying for 20 years. After I made this difficult choice, someone suggested that I needed to give my birth mother another "chance" because she probably has many regrets in her life. After so many years worth of chances, I can't put myself through this anymore.

I never realized how angry I was, and still am, with my birth mother. I have often wondered if she had been a young teenage girl in 1968, instead of an adult woman at 33 years old, if I would be so upset with her. No, I don't have any regrets searching for and meeting my birth mother. I would do it all over again, however, there are many things I would do differently.

Search and reunion is such an emotional journey. Sometimes wonderful relationships are made and other times the relationships sour quickly. I wholeheartedly support my fellow adoptees in any way I can who want to search, who have searched, or who aren't sure what they want to do.

Adoption is a life-long journey. It's not about the adoptive parents, the courts, the adoption agencies, or my birth mother who wants nothing to do with me. Adoption is about the adoptee. What I am determined to accomplish in my life now is to be an advocate for adoptees and stress that prospective adoptive parents NEED training – adopted children want and need to talk about their birth parents.

Tips for Reunion

Take it slow, one day at a time.

Don't feel guilty or ashamed or ungrateful! You have a right to reunite with your birth family.

Find an adoption support group and talk to others who have been or are in reunion.

Expect an emotional roller coaster ride – being prepared for a wide range of emotions, helps.

Give the relationship time.

Be patient – keep in mind that this is new to both of you.

Be honest.

Set limits and boundaries. You don't have to spend every waking or free moment with your birth family.

Don't push too hard.

Be respectful.

My name is **Holly Watson**, an adult adoptee from NW Pennsylvania, who was adopted at 6 days old. I am a wife, a mother, and a Grammy to three princesses and a handsome prince. I am the founder of Open Line Adoption Connection, a support group for adult adoptees who are searching or who have searched.

I am also a Pennsylvania rep for American Adoption Congress and an adoptee activist who believes adult adoptees should have access to their original birth certificates. One thing that I am determined to do in my life is to advocate for adoptees and to stress that prospective adoptive parents NEED training and adopted children WANT and need to talk about their first parents.

Risk and Reward

by Becky Drinnen

"Owning our story can be hard but not nearly as difficult as spending our lives running from it. Embracing our vulnerabilities is risky but not nearly as dangerous as giving up on love and belonging and joy – the experiences that make us the most vulnerable. Only when we are brave enough to explore the darkness will we discover the infinite power of our light." – Brene Brown

On a recent camping vacation, I spoke briefly to a young couple that was in their fourth month of traveling cross-country on their mopeds. I was intrigued by our brief interaction and I find myself wishing there had been an opportunity to ask them more questions about their journey. And I find myself wondering about how the rest of their trip will go.

How is this connected to adoption? In the grand scheme of things, I may occasionally think of this couple when I see a moped or meet someone from southwestern Oregon. The fact that I will never know more about them will not impact my life in a significant way. On the other hand, another couple did have a significant impact on who I am.

I share my parents' DNA. Yet some would say that doesn't matter for those who are adopted. In fact, society and current laws in many states are set up to ensure that adoptees have no more access to information about the people who created them than I will have about this couple I spoke to for a few brief moments.

This fact is incredibly frustrating to me and many other adoptees. We have a choice to make. We can allow ourselves to play the victim. Or we can take action, in some fashion, to make an impact and effect change. We can become advocates for change. We can educate ourselves and help others affected by adoption. We can share our experiences with others in hopes of changing. And we can look for any possible opportunity to change our own individual situation.

I had a privilege many adoptees do not. Because of the way Ohio law was written, I was able to access my original birth certificate and therefore locate the mother who birthed me when I was in my early twenties. I realize how fortunate I am that I did not have to fight for the right to access MY birth certificate. However, finding did not equal reunion. My mother was not open to reunion. Though I had some limited contact with her sister, my aunt, I did not have near the information I longed for.

For over twenty years, I mourned the fact that I would never know those things I longed to know. Telling myself I was fine with the way things stood did not work. I would successfully stuff my "adoption stuff" for a year or two before something would trigger an obsession with all things adoption. In time, I would once again manage to stuff the reality of my adoption down deep. This is clearly not healthy in any way.

Three or so years ago, I decided I was no longer willing to subvert my needs to my mother's wishes. After weeks of working up my nerve, I called her. This time, twenty-some years after I first contacted her, she was willing to have a conversation with me. I learned many of the things I wanted to know. We had a great conversation, but we have had only limited email contact since.

Though it is not the reunion I had hoped for, my one conversation with my mother was very healing for me. And I think for her, as well.

I would not have had this experience if I had accepted the status quo.

One thing I did not learn in our conversation was the name of my father. The answer to this question was one piece of information I wanted badly to learn when we spoke. Knowing about my mother was incredibly important – she carried me for nine months, after all. However, I got exactly half of my DNA from her. The rest came from my father. I knew I was a blend of both of them and I wanted to know about them both.

Years before, my aunt gave me a few details about where and how he and my mother met – along with her opinion that he was a "bad person". The scant paragraphs from the adoption agency gave me a few more facts about ethnic heritage and occupation. And my mother gave me her story, but not a name.

My longing to know my entire story did not end when I spoke with my mother. I was incredibly frustrated with my inability to know about this important piece of my heritage. No unsealing of records in the world would give me that name. His name was not on my birth certificate. It may or may not have been in adoption agency records. The only person I knew who could give me that name was my mother.

I had information, but I didn't think I had anything that would lead me to a real person. Just words on a piece of paper.

- I knew the state he lived in at the time of my birth.

- I knew his occupation, and the occupation of his father.

- I knew how my parents met.

- I had ethnic background and a basic physical description.

Not much to go on, right? Not willing to take no for an answer, I decided to see what I could learn. I felt like I was looking for a needle in a haystack, but I knew one thing for sure. If I didn't try I had exactly a zero percent chance of success. Here's what I did next:

- I searched census records to get the name of the relative my mother was visiting when my parents met.

- I found her obituary record, and with it the names of her family members and where she lived. Through publicly available records, I was able to determine where she lived at the time my parents met.

- I searched an index of newspapers in the town where the relative lived for any and every mention of family members.

It was as simple and as complicated as that. I can still see myself sitting at my desk eating lunch when I opened the email containing the full newspaper articles I had requested from the library. One article I had been particularly interested in seeing was a wedding announcement for my mother's cousin. And just like that, there it was. What I had been seeking. My mother was a bridesmaid. And the date of the wedding corresponded with the time my parents would have met, if what I had been told was correct.

I knew my search was paying off. Gut instinct and a quick review of everything I knew told me that this wedding announcement held the key to learning the identity of my father.

My next step was to research every male member of the bridal party. I learned enough to rule out all except one. After looking at everything I could find about the best man in this wedding, I was confident I had found my father. Not confident enough, though, to call and announce myself.

Instead, after weeks of working up enough nerve, I called the bride, my mother's cousin. After shaking off her surprise, she gave me the name of my father. I. Was. Right. My new cousin was so generous with her words. She was so open to a phone call that caught her completely off guard. With her words, she gave me the gift of knowledge. And more.

In the space of a short phone call, words on a piece of paper became flesh and blood. Soon after our phone call ended, I received an email from my new relative. A photo from her wedding. Right on my computer screen – both of my parents in the same photo. That which had been hidden was right before my eyes.

There you have it. Non-identifying information, along with an Ancestry.com subscription. A newspaper microfilm index and hours upon hours of search time. Someone who knew I existed and didn't believe keeping a secret trumped my right to know. All that and a healthy dose of adoptee intuition led me to the name of my father. A name I was never supposed to know.

After celebrating my success, though, I realized my search was only half over. My father was still alive. I have brothers and sisters. I had been able to put together more information that many adoptees are able to learn. But I still didn't know if meeting my father was an option.

The only way I was going to know if my father was willing to meet was to ask. Once again I found myself working up enough nerve to make a phone call. After a few misses, I was able to connect with my father. That phone call didn't go well. I wasn't sure if he was avoiding my questions, or if he wasn't clear what I was asking. I ended the call before I asked if he was my father.

After coming so close, I wasn't willing to just let this go. It was too important. Over the following months, I debated endlessly over my next steps.

Thanks to Google News Alerts, I was able to determine where I might be able to see and possibly meet my father in a public place. I wasn't sure I would have the nerve to do this, but here's where the adoptee community is such a valuable resource for adoptees. I had shared details of my search with other adoptees. One of those adoptees had shared her bold move – knocking on her mother's door to introduce herself. Another encouraged me to be bold and introduce myself.

After a great deal of soul searching, prayer and discussion, my husband and I made the drive to the place where I might have grown up, had I been raised by my birth family.

Within fifteen minutes of arriving at the event I thought my father would attend, I found him. An hour or so later, he was by himself. With my husband's encouragement, I introduced myself to him.

Amazingly, his words were something like: "I think we need to sit down and talk about this". And that's exactly what we did. That first meeting was over a year ago. Since that time, we have confirmed our relationship via DNA. We have slowly gotten to know each other through regular phone conversations. I have more information about by family history than I ever imagined possible. And, I have met two brothers and a sister, along with an aunt, nieces and nephews and cousins. I have attended church with my father and had dinner in his home.

Had I accepted my initial belief – and what adoption agencies and gatekeepers would have me believe – that there was no way possible for me to learn the identity of my father unless my mother gave me his name, I would still be completely in the dark. And a relationship that has given me the gift of a big piece of my identity would have never happened.

The moral of this story is – take charge, do what you can. Through action there is an opportunity for healing. Don't take no for an answer. Don't assume that what you desire is not possible. By taking risks, I have gained more than I ever thought possible on that day long ago when I first realized that my mother did not want a relationship with me. By taking those risks and taking steps that have led me toward learning more about my identity and my family, I gained much more than information. I gained confidence in my abilities and myself. And I found family.

Becky Drinnen is an Ohio, Baby Scoop Era adoptee who searched for and found her birth parents. She is also an advocate for adoptee rights and a co-facilitator for Adoption Network Cleveland's general discussion group.

Becky works in corporate America and loves her role as a wife, mom and grandma. In her free time, you'll find her immersed in genealogy research, reading a good book, or enjoying the great outdoors. Becky blogs about adoption at puzzlesandpossibilities.com and is a contributor to *Adoption Reunion in the Social Media Age*, edited by Laura Dennis.

PART IV: SURVIVING REJECTION

Funeral Crashing, or "How Far Will You Go"

by Elle Cuardaigh

"It is easier for a father to have children than for children to have a real father." – Pope John XXIII

I was twenty-two, married, and had been in reunion with my birth mother for a year when I first attempted contact with my birth father. He didn't know about me. My mother left town without telling him, because she didn't want him further involved, but mostly because she didn't want to hurt his wife. She really liked his wife. "She was nice," Pamela remembered, thoughtfully, leaving me with the distinct impression Glenn Havner was not. She also remembered Shirley as smart, so I would need to be careful in how I approached, to be able to do it without her knowing. "Information, not confrontation," became my mantra. I did not want to shock him or hurt him, but even more, I wanted to protect her. It was important to Pamela, so it was important to me.

I tried registered mail, regular mail, and phone, and was met with a wall of silence each time. The phone call was first. We had a terse, pointless exchange before he hung up on me. I think he was drunk. He certainly was rude, and not knowing who I was or why I was calling, there was no justification for it. The registered letter followed, with photos, sent to his place of employment. In the letter I told him plainly who I was and who my mother was. The photos alone should have been proof enough I was telling the truth. No response. Never a response.

I always made sure to circumvent Shirley. And I made it plain in my letters that I wasn't looking for public recognition or a relationship. I was so considerate. I even created a "fill in the blank" questionnaire to send back to me regarding medical history. But he didn't even do that. The only acknowledgement were the two slips of green paper where he signed for my first letter and photos. I kept them because they were all I had.

For the next year or so I sent a short note every time I moved or changed phone numbers, just to remind him I was there. Always very casual, nothing threatening. He never had reason to believe I'd show up on his doorstep. Since he lived in southern Idaho while I lived in western Washington, there was no reason for him to worry about running into me. But even with the safe distance, he never answered.

I wasn't done, though. I ordered his birth certificate. Armed with that information, plus everything my mother remembered about him (I was lucky in that she was always forthcoming), an adoptee friend and I travelled to the little town in northern Idaho where my parents met, so we could do some "sleuthing." Jenny and I had some experience with sleuthing, since we rooted out her unwilling birth mother the year before. I had found some of my siblings' names in City Directories but none of them lived in Coeur D'Alene any longer; the whole family moved to Boise decades earlier. So I wasn't concerned about coming face to face with Glenn or Shirley or any of my half-siblings. I never would have attempted this if they still lived there. As always, I was protecting them. From me.

We drove through the old downtown of Coeur D'Alene and in the surrounding neighborhood to see if we spotted anyone who looked as if they might be a relative. I had found in previous research that my grandmother's extended family still resided there, so I had some addresses to cruise past. I had no actual plan, since nothing ever went according to plan anyway. We checked the local school and landmarks. Then we came across the oldest-looking Catholic church in town. Jenny and I looked at each other. "Church records!" we said in unison.

We went in to find a pleasant middle-aged woman in the office. "I'm doing genealogy research for my mother," I explained, smiling. I knew to keep it simple and smile in order to get cooperation. "She told me if I was ever passing through to try to look this person up: Glenn Havner."

"Glenn Havner? Sure, I know him," she said brightly. "My husband and I go fishing with him and Shirley nearly every summer."

I resisted a strong urge to bolt.

"Really? That's...great," I said, managing to keep smiling. "So you can tell me something about his family—"

"Wait. How are you related to him?"

"Hm? Oh, distantly." (Tacoma and Coeur D'Alene are very distant from each another.) "I've never met him."

"But your mother wants you to research his family?"

"Yes, she's quite obsessed with genealogy. You know how some people get." I gave Jenny a knowing glance. She smiled and nodded in agreement. "Well, some relatives live right down the street. Bill and Cathy. Really nice people. I'll just call—" she said, reaching for the phone.

"No! I don't want to bother anyone. Anyone else. Since you know Glenn and Shirley, that's perfect. I was just wondering what's in the records?" Oh-God-please-put-the-phone-down-I'm-so-close.

She gave me a curious look but put the phone back in its cradle. Please do not notice the obvious resemblance, I prayed. Jenny sat in the chair next to mine, casually poised like this was the most normal thing in the world. I tried to copy her relaxed appearance.

"And you want information about his family?"

"Yes, and anyone related to him. My mother wasn't quite clear on the lineage so I'd better just get everything so I don't miss anyone. We came all the way from Tacoma and won't pass through here again."

This must have sounded crazy enough to be plausible because she got out the record books. As she went through them page by page, year by year, I wrote in my notebook at a furious pace. She explained as she went:

"Glenn's younger sister is Jean. Glenn's daughter Heather Jean is named after her. I can't remember Heather's last name – she's been married a few years now." Heather. My sister's name is Heather. I recorded her date of birth.

She gave two more names with birth dates. My younger siblings, Kelli and David. Another sister – I couldn't believe my luck. I must have been speaking with David the time I called anonymously to see if Shirley and Glenn were still married. Eldest were Ryan and Joseph. Heather came next. Then me.

"Shirley wasn't Catholic before they got married," the secretary informed me. She was pregnant though. I knew that from Pamela. Shirley must have told her, or maybe Glenn did. Suddenly the secretary looked up and said:

"Do you want to know about Shirley's family too?"

"Sure," I replied, thinking it would look suspicious to say anything else.

She rattled off the names of her parents and siblings and other factoids.

"Do you know anything about Glenn's father's family?" I asked.
"No, but you know what? Bill and Cathy would know. Let me just give them a call," she said, reaching for the phone.

"No. Really. We don't want to bother them. And," looking at my watch, "gosh, look at the time. We need to go. Long drive. Thank you so much for all your help."

Jenny floored it out of town.

When the laughter finally died down at the next search and reunion meeting, someone said (wiping tears from their eyes) the church secretary will no doubt tell Glenn and Shirley, so then what? Maybe this will jolt him into contacting me, I reasoned, just to keep me from actually showing up in Boise. I wouldn't actually do that, but he didn't know.

But as before, there was no phone call. There was no letter. Using my list-making skills from childhood I dissected all the information I had and created a family tree, listing all my siblings – adopted, step and birth – in family groups and chronological order. I looked them up in City Directories, sometimes discovering spouses or new jobs. I remembered their birthdays and kept them in my prayers. I held onto these scraps of info like they were precious clues to a mystery. Because that's all I had, really: names, dates and theories.

Years went by. I stopped trying to contact my birth father. I was busy with life in general, but it wasn't just that. I felt he didn't deserve to know his grandchildren. If he wouldn't acknowledge me, he didn't deserve to know them.

One summer when the kids were small, there was a tragic story on the evening news, of a young man who died while camping. Slipped and hit his head on a rock. He looked so athletic and handsome in his photo; it was hard to believe he could die from a simple fall. Something made me go back to the story again and again. Then I read his obituary and understood.

He was Shirley Havner's nephew. The church secretary in Idaho gave me the names of Shirley's siblings but not their locations. One apparently lived here in the Tacoma area and this was a son. My mind raced.

Had Glenn and Shirley visited here before? Would they come now? It had been more than ten years since I first contacted my birth father. I never told him I moved to Tacoma, never told him how much I knew about his family.

I called my mother, Pamela.

"Could you watch the kids for me? I need to crash a funeral."

I dressed in a nice black skirt and beige jacket. I wanted to arrive just before it started, so if Glenn noticed me he wouldn't have time to bail. I had no plan in mind. Nothing ever went according to plan anyway.

At the funeral home, I asked where Mike's service was being held. The woman at the desk said it started in the chapel in ten minutes, but would I like to view the body first?

Didn't expect that. Heard myself say, "Yes, of course," and next thing I knew I was alone in a darkened room with the body of someone I had never met.

I suppose I should have expected to be punished somehow, I thought ruefully, and approached the open casket to gaze at this stranger's face: Young. Handsome. Should be alive. I wondered what he would have accomplished had he not gone on that camping trip. I wondered if it mattered, if this was just "his time" and would have died regardless. I wondered why things happen the way they do. I apologized to him silently for being there with ulterior motives and departed.

The chapel was standing room only. This worked well for me because I was forced to stand in the back where I had a view of everyone, even if it was just the back of their heads. In the front rows sat the family. I examined everyone. That must be his father. That must be his mother...one by one, row by row. About the third row back I stopped. There was a man about the right age with dark silky hair. Is that him? Is that Shirley sitting next to him? There was no way to know from my vantage point. With the crowd, I wasn't sure there would be a way for me to maneuver to see his face.

But the opportunity presented itself. When the service concluded we were invited to pay our respects to the family, starting with those standing in the back. The rest were asked to remain seated, i.e. trapped. I walked to the front and joined the line of mourners leaning over to talk quietly to Mike's family in the front row.

Waiting my turn, I casually looked up to where I thought I saw Glenn and Shirley from the back of the room and locked eyes with a couple staring at me in utter shock. She was a beautiful blonde. He was me, only thirty years older and male. They could not look away and I resisted the urge to do just that, forcing myself to level my gaze into theirs. They didn't move – didn't even look like they were breathing – just sat frozen as if seeing a ghost.

Only a moment had passed, but it was my turn to give my regards. Offering my hand, I murmured my condolences and walked through the adjacent door leading outside.

It was over. Nothing had happened yet everything had happened. I went to retrieve the children.

"How did he look?" Pamela asked with great curiosity.

"Older. A lot more mellow. And…surprised."   But their matching expressions gave me some information: Shirley knew. She knew about me. I was not The Secret, I was The One We Don't Talk About. He must have shown her the photos and letters because it wasn't just shock, it was the shock of recognition. They knew me. The only other possibility was that she saw the resemblance, but if that was the case she would have nudged Glenn and pointed me out. Instead they sat as if pretending to be invisible – like deer in the forest – hoping I wouldn't see them.

She knew. All this time I had been protecting her, and she knew. I had been so careful, so considerate, not only for her sake, but for their children, my brothers and sisters. Protecting them from what? Me? If someone told me twelve years earlier that I would crash a funeral to see my birth father, I would have told them they were crazy. But being rejected, over and over – with silence – not even a "Drop dead," pushed me up against a wall. In the end, I was willing to do anything.

I wanted to see my father in the flesh, just once. I got what I wanted.

Reunion/Rejection survival tips:

1. Know what you want.
2. Always go with your gut instincts.
3. Have no regrets.

> "Security is mostly a superstition. It does not exist in nature, nor do the children of men as a whole experience it. Avoiding danger is no safer in the long run than outright exposure. Life is either a daring adventure, or nothing."
> ~Helen Keller

Elle Cuardaigh was born in Tacoma, Washington and has vowed to never leave the beautiful Pacific Northwest. Using a nom de plume, Elle lives her secret life as a writer while simultaneously juggling the responsibilities of being mother, daughter, and sister to many.

Author of *The Tangled Red Thread* (An Da Shealladh 2014, through amazon.com) and blog ellecuardaigh.com (WordPress), Elle focuses on spirituality in adoption/reunion and as a writer has long been a supporter of adoptee rights and adoption reform.

Discovering the Real Me

by Lisa Floyd

My journey would not have been possible had I not located my birth family and found the answer to questions about the beginning of my life. I was not a blank slate who could just learn to adapt to my surroundings and forget about my birth family. I repressed all the difficult and painful emotions and retreated into myself with sky-high walls that no one could penetrate. For decades, I believed I was okay with my adoption experience and was blissful in my fog. It was not until I turned forty that I really began to wonder about my birth family. It took another year before I worked up the courage to contact my birth mother through an intermediary.

When she refused contact, the world as I knew it came crashing down. I had always felt unwanted and like I was a mistake, but her secondary rejection just seemed to confirm these beliefs for me. I wondered what I had done to deserve such treatment. I began the very long and arduous task of grieving her loss, which I would not wish on my worst enemy. It was the most painful time of my life, and I would bounce between grief that would have me sobbing uncontrollably, to being filled with rage that I had not experienced before. I did not see an end in sight and really believed that things would not ever get better. This process lasted for two years. I thought it would destroy me, but it only made me stronger.

I decided to try to locate my birth family in August of last year, and I was able to do that with the help of an amazing search angel. I knew my birth mother wanted nothing to do with me, but I wanted to try to contact my four siblings. I sent them certified letters telling them that I believed I was their sister and would like a chance to get to know them. One brother immediately responded, and we have been in reunion ever since. The other three refuse contact at this time, and I respect their wishes. My brother and his family have been very welcoming and given me the sense of connection that I never had before.

I had a wonderful upbringing with my parents that was filled with love, but I needed to search to find out who I am and where I come from. I realized I could not move forward when I did not know what had happened in the beginning of my life. Reunion has not healed all of my adoption wounds. In fact, it brought on more rejection by my siblings and eventually my birth mother when she found out that I had made contact with her children. I found dysfunction and details that were difficult to accept, but I have no regrets because I know my truth. I now have a foundation upon which I can build my life.

Reunion is an emotional roller-coaster hard to prepare for, but it helped me to have the support of my adoptive parents and the adoptee community that I discovered through social media.

The biggest piece of advice I have for anyone contemplating reunion is to not have expectations that are set too high. I did this with my brother and it caused some problems in our relationship. Reunions are emotionally charged for everyone, and I believe it is best to give the other person the time and space he or she needs in order to process all of the various emotions. Adoptees can be so hungry for the connection with flesh and blood relatives that we have never had. We must remember that our birth families grew up together with the benefit of genetic mirroring (seeing themselves reflected in other family members) so maintaining a relationship with you may not be a high priority for them. Connections to us may not have the same significance for them which can trigger feelings of rejection if they do not contact us as often as we think they should. It does not mean they do not care. They are just being who they are and relating as they always have to others.

It requires time and effort to build any relationship, and it takes even more effort to build a relationship with reunited birth family members. I try to remember this with my brother, and I am enjoying getting to know him. It is usually up to me to initiate contact and keep the relationship moving ahead. It may not be fair, but that is just the way it is. I have learned to do this with my brother, and it is worth it to have him in my life. Reunion is not easy, but it is worth the sacrifice and effort.

I look at my life now compared to where I was two years ago, and I sit in awe at how much I have changed. There is no magic cure for healing of my adoption wounds. Popping a pill did not help. I had to go through the almost unbearable pain of dealing with all the emotions I had repressed for so many years. Things did not immediately change, because I still did not have a clue who I was. I have not had trauma therapy to address my issues although I would like to one day, but I do know my Lord and Savior Jesus Christ. I know beyond the shadow of a doubt that He has orchestrated every last detail of my life and brought everything into place at just the right time.

My birth mother passed away last month without ever allowing me to meet her, and her last request was that I not be allowed to attend the funeral. I was devastated, but I realize she could not open herself up to the pain and trauma that she had buried all those years ago. I was able to visit her grave, and I have forgiven her and have closure. I only wish she had healing and closure in her lifetime. Her decision to relinquish me had a negative impact on all my siblings, and I only hope one day we can know one another. I cannot imagine what it must have been like for them to have a sibling who never came home from the hospital and to wonder if it could have been them instead.

With her death, I have been able to obtain a copy of my original birth certificate and get all of my identifying information from the state of Indiana. I now know where I was for the first nine days of my life, and I was even able to see the foster home where I spent five days. I have documents that show tangible evidence of the first days of my life, and they have given me a sense of being real for the first time in my life. These things may not mean much to most people, but they mean the world to me. It is only in connecting with my past and my birth family that I have been able to connect with myself and form my identity. I have found my authentic self, and I am ready to thrive. I look at my life, and I realize that I am a miracle. It is only through the glory of God that I am experiencing my healing and redemption.

I have recently been able to connect with my deceased birth father's brother and wife, and they are excited to get to know me and have already told me that I am a member of their family. It is a very different reaction than I got from my birth mother's family, but I look forward to developing a relationship with them. They want to know me, and they had been expecting a call from me all these years. They knew about the pregnancy, but they knew nothing about what happened to me. I am amazed at all I have been able to discover, and I cannot wait to see what else will happen.

The process of facing adoption-related trauma and emotions is not easy, but I needed to do it in order to heal from the pain of the past. Adoptees are beyond strong to have survived all that we have, and the feelings will not kill us even if it feels like they will. It is only in facing those difficult things that we find our true strength and authentic selves. I have found healing in writing and rediscovered a love I had not experienced in years. I will be pursuing my God-given calling to become an adoption therapist to counsel my fellow adoptees, and this would not have happened had I not been willing to stare darkness in the face. Those very dark places created a beauty and empathy in me, and I hope to help other adoptees find this place in themselves. Healing is possible, and we owe it to ourselves to discover it.

I sit here in amazement as I recall the past eight months of my life. There have been a lot of wonderful highs and some very heart-breaking and painful lows, but I regret nothing I have gone through because I now have an accurate picture of who I am.

Here are the survival tips I have for any adoptee who is struggling with adoption issues or is trying to navigate reunion:

1. It is imperative to have an active support system whether it is family, friends or a trusted confidante. I discovered the adoptee community on social media, and they quite literally helped me keep my sanity. I found support, encouragement, and validation. I have also made some good friendships which I value. There are many good adoption-related groups on Facebook if one needs support, and many of the groups are closed for added protection.

2. I cannot stress the importance of taking care of yourself when you are going through a rough time processing difficult emotions. I will honestly say that I had so little regard for myself that self-care was almost non-existent, but I gained the understanding that I am worthy and deserving of being good to myself. This shift in mindset occurred when my self-esteem increased. I am careful to get enough rest, eat properly, and exercise. I want to function at my best physically, mentally, spiritually, and emotionally. I think it is vitally important to speak to yourself in a kind manner. You are worthy of dignity and self-respect and expect nothing less!

3. Do not expect too much of others in the initial stages of reunion. High expectations can kill a relationship and cause lots of hurt feelings. Reunions are a time of adjustment for everyone, and people need time to process everything that is going on. I do not have the luxury of having a shared history with my brother so we just have to start from scratch and develop our relationship from where we are. It takes time and patience to get to know the other person and develop a closer relationship.

4. Be patient with yourself and everyone else involved in reunion. The last eight months have been crazy for me, my birth family, and my adoptive family. It has been a time of great change, and it helps me to consider the ways in which this has affected others that I love. This aids me in understanding them and their perspectives better. We cannot predict how others will react, especially under emotional stress, so it is good to try to give them the benefit of the doubt. I have learned we all make mistakes and not to take things too seriously. I have had so much to process, and I focus on taking care of myself and loving the others who I have in my life. Reunion and adoption issues can feel like landmines, but they can be handled with dignity and grace.

Lisa Floyd grew up in Indiana in a closed adoption wondering who she was and where she came from. It took many years for her adoption fog to emerge after which she decided to search for and eventually reunite with both sides of her birth families. It is only in finding her birth families and what occurred in the beginning days of her life that she has found her identity and her voice.

She is passionate about adoptee rights and plans on becoming an attachment and trauma therapist to help her fellow adoptees find their authentic selves and meaningful, purpose-filled lives. She is also a contributing writer in the adoption anthology *Adoption Therapy: Perspectives from Clients and Clinicians on Processing and Healing Post-Adoption Issues.*

Better Than Nothing

by Sophi Fletcher

Finding biological relatives for the first time can be life-changing for an adoptee, if one has never known a single person they are related to, act, or look like.

In spite of repeated rejection, obstacles, and adversity, I would advise anyone searching to never give up looking for the answers you need. If I had given up, I would never have found or met some of the most loving and accepting cousins I could ever hope for, nor could I explain my many "unique" interests and traits.

Apparently I have always wanted to know who I am. I grew up knowing I was adopted, before I consciously remember being told. Even though it was not a secret, the word always stuck in my throat when I had to tell someone that I was adopted.

I remember when I was only 13 watching a "made for TV" movie called "The Stranger Who Looks Like Me," starring Beau Bridges and Meredith Baxter as college-age adoptees looking for their birth families. I never forgot that movie and the impact it had on me, nor did I ever stop looking for it on video. It wasn't until just a few years ago that I finally found a copy online and bought it immediately. It was well worth the $20.00 and I would have paid more, just to watch it again. I believe the realistic situations that were presented helped to prepare me for my own less than "happy Oprah reunion" search down the road. It was a telling moment when I was able to recite a particular line from the movie as I watched it again, so many years later.

I felt like a square peg in a round hole much of my life, never really bonding with my adoptive parents, who were quite a bit older when they adopted me, (my adoptive dad was sometimes mistaken for my grandfather, to his embarrassment and my own) having few close friends, but always seeking affection and affirmation from many males in my life. According to my late adoptive father, some of my first words were, "Weave me awone" (Leave me alone) when he would try to play with me.

When I was 17, my adoptive father requested information from the attorney that handled my private adoption in Bakersfield, CA. I have this brief clearing of the fog in my mind, like seeing a picture of me holding the letter for which he paid $85.00 (a goodly sum in 1978) which provided the name, date of birth, level of education, number of other children, and even a street address, for my biological mother! (Nothing about my father, however. I'll get to him later.) Shortly after that – it seems like it might have even been the same day– we received a call from her, in which she told my dad in no uncertain terms that she wanted no contact from any of us with her or "her" family. That made it quite clear that I was not a part of that family, nor ever would be.

I began doing genealogy before I knew there was a name for it. We lived only an hour away from the place where I was born, so the local public library had city directories for Bakersfield, which was where I began my investigation into who my older half-siblings might be. For those unfamiliar with this resource, years ago it was common for these Polk directories to be published, at least for larger cities, which listed people by name, address and occupation vs. just a telephone directory. I found several males listed as "student" under the name I was researching, and I remember just trying to digest the information. These names suddenly became more real to me. I had brothers, older brothers, who were students, like me. In retrospect, I'm thinking the directories must have been several years old, because I was in high school myself at the time, and they were 6, 10 and 12 years older than me.

I seem to have inherited my birth mother's stubborn streak, because I have never stopped searching, except for some stretches of time to regroup, and I never will. After many fits and starts, well before the internet was available, I would copy phone numbers from phone books at the library and cold call people with the same last name as my half-brothers in various towns throughout California. Some of you know how difficult just picking up the telephone can be in this situation, so years could pass between phone calls from the same list.

In the spring of 1988, I hit pay dirt when the wife of one of my twin half-brothers answered the phone. It was such a shock and an emotional moment when I told her who I was, that we both agreed to hang up and call back in half an hour. She shared a lot of wonderful information with me about family traits and talents, family dynamics, etc. and it was like cracking open a window to who I might have been. However, that was as far as it went. Her husband merely asked her what I wanted from him/them, and had no interest in speaking to me, let alone meeting me.

On the first Saturday in July of that year, I was jarred out of my comfort zone when I answered the phone, expecting a man I had just started dating to say when he was coming to pick me up for church, but instead, it was my birth mother, and it was not a social call.

She had found out from her son's wife that I had made contact, and said that she told my father years ago that she wanted no contact from me or us with her family. She asked if I had ever been raped, and claimed that was how I came to be, and topped it off by saying, "If abortion was legal, I would have had one." Ouch. In retrospect, I think of how very ridiculous that statement was. If you had had one, obviously we wouldn't be having this conversation, but she said it to be hurtful, and hurtful it was.

My new friend/boyfriend did come to take me to church but I was in a daze the rest of the day, in shock from such an onslaught from the one who brought me into this world. I had been out of college a few years by then, and the only friends I had lived far away, so this man was the closest refuge I had. I had very little self-confidence and went on to make a series of mistakes, first moving in with him, giving up a perfect and affordable apartment in St. Helena, (Napa Valley) and then went on to marry him, as I felt I couldn't go back or be financially self-sufficient.

He turned out to have some issues with alcohol and his sexual identity, and we divorced in 1994. I went to an AA dance to meet someone sober, and began to date someone a little too new to recovery to be any healthier than the ex. However, at one point, this man took me to Bakersfield, where I was born, where I got to look at high school yearbooks in the public library, and I saw pictures of my brothers for the first time. I was particularly struck by the fact that the older two were very involved in activities and appeared happy and smiling in their various photos, while the younger twins were quite somber and not involved in extracurricular activities. They were also very different in looks and complexion. (There have been rumors that the father of the twins may not have been the man my birth mother was married to either).

After I divorced, I moved to Oakland, CA for a job in The City (San Francisco). I purchased my first laptop computer (as a full-sized one would not fit in my studio apartment!) and thus began my online introduction to genealogy and adoption support. I attended a few genealogy conferences and classes, and somehow found out about the wealth of information available through the Family History Centers of the Mormon Church.

I had determined that if I couldn't move "forward" with my birth mother, I would then go "backwards" to find out who I was and where we came from. Through census records, I discovered that my mother was born in Oklahoma, which was hard enough for this California girl to wrap my mind around, until I went back another decade and learned that her father, my grandfather, was born in Georgia. This was indeed a paradigm shift.

With the help of volunteers at the Family History Center, and just plain persistence, I began to gather the details of my life and form an incomplete picture of my family and my past.

Rootsweb was one of the first sites I remember using, where one could list the surnames they were researching, and compare them to other researchers, who were available to contact through email. There were also things called message boards, where I met some of the nicest people, who turned out to be cousins of mine. Unlike my immediate family, these folks didn't care how I got here, they just called me family and showed me love and acceptance.

One particular line was that of my g-g-grandmother, Easter Fletcher, and it was her maiden name that I chose when I felt it was time to change my name and reclaim a part of myself. I went to court and filed the necessary papers, paid about $200.00, and became Dorothy Fletcher in 1999.

As is typical with "the fog", some of the details escape me, as does the actual order of who I found first, but after more detective work in the mid-90s, I found my birth mother's sister in Northern California, who denied my existence the first time we spoke on the phone. However, somewhere within that same time frame, I also found her son (my 1st cousin) living 10 minutes away from me in Oakland! (One of the many stories you hear about adoption synchronicity).

When I went to his house to meet my first cousin for the first time, his first words were, "You look just like her." (I have gotten that from the cousins several times). I had learned from the sister- in-law that I spoke to back in '88 that photography was one of the family traits that I shared, so I carried with me what I felt was the best photo I had taken, of an orchid with a rough redwood tree trunk behind it, and discovered that we not only had photography in common, we both had a very similar eye for composition! That was one of many "puzzle pieces" of ME that I have gathered close to my heart over the years.

My first cousin then spoke to his mother, my aunt, and convinced her of my truth and existence, and took me up to meet her and her husband for a weekend. It was one of a handful of moments in life that I would describe as truly life-changing. There have been few moments in my life in which I felt true, deep, abiding joy...but that was one of them. I couldn't stop smiling as I was introduced to their other son and a daughter. My uncle became something of an advocate for me while my aunt was reticent, due to her relationship with her sister, my birth mother.

As is often the case with relative-strangers, the other son and I sized each other up and there was a definite attraction—for about a minute—and we were both brought up short by the realization that we are, in fact, first cousins!

Around this same time, I managed to find my oldest half-brother in San Jose, after somehow learning he had "gone to college there." I may have jumped to conclusions, e.g. "Let's see, he's from Bakersfield. San Jose has Stanford and SJ State. I'm going to go with State." I guessed right! I contacted their alumni association, where I reached a very nice lady, who was so sympathetic to my request, and wanted to help me, but "privacy" had already kicked in, and she couldn't just tell me outright. A couple of times she said something like, "He's here," but I didn't pick up on it until after I hung up the phone. I called her right back and I said, "Wait, he's "here" as in, in this (the 408) area code??" And she said yes!

I then found myself at the San Jose library, where I checked property records, thinking at his age, he might own a house. I found a phone number and cross-referenced it to get the address, right there in San Jose. The same boyfriend who accompanied me to Bakersfield took me there, to look in the face of my closest relative so far. It was late in the afternoon when we went up to his door. He opened it, and I told him I thought I was his sister. A variety of emotions darted across his face, including shock, disbelief, and a smile of welcome. He invited me in and we began the awkward process of introductions. I had brought my adoption papers with our mother's signature on them as proof of my claims.

After his wife looked them over, she actually cried – but not for joy. She mumbled something about a long-lost uncle having appeared in their family who was not welcome either. To this day, I am bewildered by her response, but I can only speculate that she saw her sainted mother-in-law falling off her pedestal with this revelation, of having a child out of wedlock and then adopting me out.

My oldest brother was very kind, and made a point of telling me the names of our grandmother and great-grandmother, who were Cherokee, and how to get a tribal membership card. What a gift from a man I only met one time. Their teenage son made a brief appearance, and we were introduced as "friends of the family." My brother and I had a couple photos taken together, and as we stood beside each other, I marveled at our similarities....our build, our naturally wavy hair, even our acne scarred faces. Awhile later, as the boyfriend and I walked dazedly to the car, I looked back at my brother's house and thought to myself, if this is all there ever is, it's still better than nothing.

After we left, we went to get some dinner. I remember going into the restroom in the restaurant, and actually seeing "someone" in the mirror for the first time; not just a blank slate with eyes, nose and mouth.

Sometime later, I spoke to my aunt. She said my brother had called her and told her he wanted to have a relationship with me, but just as quickly, his wife called our aunt back and said, "It's not gonna happen." Their son then emailed me a hateful, ugly message, called me a stalker, and used all kinds of filthy language. In situations like that, I can use the word "grateful"-- that I am not a part of THAT family.

I continued to pursue my genealogy, and discovered that there were cousins living in Georgia, where my birth mother's father was born. I did a lot of cold calling then, once I had a name, and left a few voicemails. I will never forget a phone call I received from a man with a very heavy Southern drawl. He said, "This uz Jurruld Blackboooorn and Ah thank we maght be rulated."

Add that to the short list of life-changing moments!

I was brought up in a Christian home, which I am thankful for, and my faith has seen me through all of these challenges and adventures. After my job in San Francisco ended, I found myself working through several temporary agencies, and assignments were sporadic at best. I felt so out of my element; driving home from high rises, industrial areas, with hundreds of other people taking up four lanes of concrete. One evening I remember hearing the country song, "Where the Green Grass Grows" on my car radio as the sun was dropping and a small flock of geese flew over in formation. I was so struck by the irony of my life at that moment, and an intense longing for change.

One of the many temp positions I held was for a company in Berkeley, setting appointments for contractors to make presentations on the newest thing in efficient windows. Sometime after that position ended, they called me back and hired me on contract, outside of the temp agency. This led to an amazing surprise, something I would refer to as a "God thing" – when the company paid out dividends, I actually received one! The amount was enough for a flight to Georgia to meet these lovely people I had only spoken to by phone. The gentleman who called me was my birth mother's second cousin, so his children are my third cousins. One of them and I share the exact same date of birth!

I booked my first cross-country flight the first part of July of 1999 from California to Atlanta. I had to change planes at Dallas-Ft. Worth, which I had never done before, and one of the Fletcher cousins I had met through the genealogy message boards came to meet me there (pre-9/11 you could still do that) and basically took me by the hand and got me to my connecting flight! We had a stranger take a picture of us, and I treasure it to this day. She was about the same age as my birth mother, but I think I look more like her in the nose and mouth than I do my own mother, which further endeared me to the Fletcher identity.

The cousins in Georgia met me at the airport, and I felt like such a dork much of the time, a fish out of water. I had made a long, comfortable tank dress to wear for travel, but it was too big, and I didn't wear a belt, and I just look ridiculous in the pictures from that time. They gave me the use of their new Eddie Bauer package Ford Explorer, and I hit the road to do research in the next county, and all the way up to North Carolina, where I had the privilege of meeting an elderly gentleman with whom I shared common great-grandparents, dating back to about 1800.

I made the trip to Georgia over the 4th of July, which held significance to me with it being one of the 13 original colonies, as I had discovered I had a few Revolutionary War Patriots in my family tree. The cousins took me to brunch at the lodge at Amicalola State Park in GA, where the Appalachian Trail begins. I gazed out over the endless misty mountains and was struck by the fact that my own Cherokee ancestors may well have stood and admired this same view. Before ever visiting GA, I watched a movie called The Education of Little Tree. Toward the end there are similar scenes of the Blue Ridge and Appalachians, and I remember sitting in my living room in Oakland, CA, and crying, saying, "I want to go home."

I fell in love with North Georgia before the plane ever landed. I made a second trip a few weeks later, and by the end of August, I had hired a disreputable moving company, (that's a whole other story) put my kitties in the car along with the T.V. and microwave, and headed east.

On the way out of California, I decided to stop at my birth mother's house. What did I have to lose? I was leaving the state so, that hot August morning in Bakersfield, I left the car running with the air conditioning on for the kitties, went to her door, and her husband answered. He didn't seem surprised, but he asked why I wanted to know. "You got a good home, didn't you," he stated, not asking, just assuming, as so many people do. I wondered if he had hired a detective to verify that somehow.

I explained what it was like to discover I have the same eye for photography as my cousin, and the same complexion and build as my oldest brother, but he didn't budge, and my mother never made an appearance. I did, however, muster my limited skills learned in an assertiveness training course, and managed, after several calm repetitions of my request, to hand him a postcard with my forwarding information on it, "just in case" she wanted it, and I was on my way.

Once in Georgia, I loved the humidity, the woods, the lightnin' bugs, the history, and being included as part of a family by the cousins down the road each Thanksgiving and Christmas....but, it never felt like a good fit; we were just too different – too much lost time and history.

While living there, I would fly out to Oregon every couple years to visit my adoptive parents, who retired in the small town I now call home. My auntie and her husband drove up from California in 2003 to meet my adoptive parents. We had a picture taken of the five of us together, with me standing in the middle of the two couples, and my head inclined toward my auntie, bringing us full circle. That uncle, my advocate, passed away not long after that special meeting, and by 2006, I found myself making another cross-country move to Oregon from Georgia to care for my elderly and increasingly-dependent adoptive parents.

God led me to a wonderful job teaching English to international high school students within walking distance of my home. My oldest half-brother taught high school English in Morgan Hill, California, for over 30 years. The aforementioned Fletcher cousin was also a teacher.

While at that job, I got a message from an adoption search/reunion site, saying someone was looking for me!! It turned out to be the sister-in-law I had found back in '88, who was no longer with my half-brother, and who wanted me to meet her/their son at some point. That never materialized, but it was an incredible feeling to have someone actually search for me, instead of the other way around.

I had my own place for the first two years, but as my adoptive parents became more dependent, I moved all three of us into a three bedroom, two bathroom, handicap-accessible apartment, where my own independence came to a grinding halt. My last trip back East was in '11, where I was able to drive up from Georgia to Essex County, Virginia (even earlier than the colonies for this history buff!) and do on-site research with an incredible volunteer doing all the leg work. The Fletcher cousin from Texas had handed over the genealogical "reins" to her nephew in New York, and he, myself and another Fletcher researcher in Georgia put our heads together and made it "over the wall" of 1786 to pre-Revolution Virginia.

That was an amazing feeling, to accomplish something that other researchers had not been able to in decades of work. This is just one example I use to encourage other searchers. Never give up! Think outside of the box! Compare notes and brainstorm.

Before the run up to Virginia, my cousin in Georgia and I spent a day together, and that felt really good. We are ten years apart in age but both have brown hair and green eyes, are single, majored in communications, and share a love for genealogy and family history. We visited the local library which has a small genealogy section, and donning white gloves, pored over old store ledgers and such, to reinforce our new discoveries.

After moving to Oregon, I visited the aunt in California a few times, before her memory issues got worse, along with those of my adoptive parents, keeping me closer to home. Over the years, she had told me that my other half-brother, one of the twins, (who does not know about me to this day – talk about a lack of communication in a family) had married a woman with kids, but they had none of their own.

My feelings toward my aunt changed drastically after learning from one of my 1st cousins that said half-brother did indeed have a daughter, and when I learned this last year, she was 18 years old. So, all these years that I have been in contact with this aunt, and her telling me that "Greg married a woman with kids but had none of his own" – were just more lies! I have not spoken to her since, as her own memory issues have increased and it would be pointless to confront her.

It was quite the deal when I did a little more detective work, online this time, and discovered a public Twitter account by said niece, and figured out who her mother is on Facebook. I read through the tweets and thought, this girl sounds like me!! I then got brave and messaged her mother on Facebook, (paid the $1.00 so it would go to her inbox and not the "other" box) held my breath, expecting either nothing, or rejection again.

But I was met with open arms and a loving heart, and someone who has known the family for many, many years, willing to share insights and history with me. She then told her daughter about me, who, after seeing my picture, remarked, "She looks just like Grandma!" (I get that a lot from that side of the family). I then took my new auntie duties seriously and let my niece know that it wasn't a good idea to have a public Twitter account. She then set it to private, and since I don't "tweet" I no longer get to see her posts.

Her mother also gave me the invaluable gift of my new first name. In the course of our getting acquainted via Facebook messaging, I posited that I had always wondered what my name might have been, had my birth mother decided to keep me. My sister-in-law didn't know the answer to that, but did know the family well enough to be able to supply two girls names that were considered before the twins were born: Cynthia and Sophia. As soon as I saw the name Sophia on my screen, I knew somehow it was mine. I've played with variations of it over the past year, and settled on Sophi. The name has very old origins, and means Wisdom, something I could have used a lot of over the years.

Once my adoptive mother is no longer with me, I will legally make the change complete. I've had some interesting responses from friends when I first tell them of the change. Almost without fail, the first thing out of their mouths is, "I never saw you as a 'Dorothy!" (Neither did I). Perhaps once I find out more about my birth father, I will select a middle name that reflects that aspect of my ancestry as well. When all is said and done, I will have gone from "Baby Girl Spain" to "Dorothy Bovee" to "Sophi Fletcher".

Thanks to social media, I've developed new and meaningful friendships on Facebook with other adoptees. It's the support group for the 21st century! So many of us are in the same boat, having faced rejection, not knowing who our mothers/fathers are, spending money and energy taking various DNA tests – all to find anyone that we can, who might know something about who we are.

I took my first DNA test in December of 2012. I discovered, to my amazement, (and yet, I had a hunch), that I was over 40% Ashkenazi Jewish! I found a male 1st cousin on my birth mother's side who was willing to test also, which gives me something to go by, to rule out her side vs. my unknown father's side.

There are little to no Jewish markers on my birth mother's side, but it confirmed my Native American ancestry, which, oddly enough, comes out of Colombia and Mexico primarily. This led to some great connections on Facebook, and to a researcher who is rewriting history as we know it, a Richard Thornton. The fact that I have Native ancestry, a Cherokee tribal membership, AND have the DNA to prove it, apparently makes me rather rare! This is truly exciting, to be a part of something so fundamental to the history of this country. What an incredible sense of belonging this sort of discovery provides.

Here is where the stories start to overlap and gather momentum. Back in the early days of the internet (or of owning personal computers, anyway) I joined what was known back in the day as a "mailing list" where folks could comment and post and only those on the list would see it. This particular list was for "adoptees who found death or rejection at the end of their search." I became friends with a gal in the UK, and we bailed from the list, which was just too dark and sad for us. We were moving on!

Our friendship continued through email, then by rare phone calls in the early 2000s as phone rates adapted and dropped for international calling, and we actually got to meet in person the first year I lived in Oregon, when she came to Portland to stay with a friend and I had a teacher's conference to attend up there.

Since then it's been more phone calls, emails, and Skype. A few years ago she jumped on the DNA testing bandwagon, while I was just biding my time as the science continued to develop (and hoping the price would drop as well!). She shared her results with me, and I remember specifically that she mentioned discovering she was part Ashkenazi Jew.

Several years went by. I finally took the Family Tree DNA (FTdna) test as a Christmas present to myself (ordered in December but the results didn't come out until after my birthday in February), and then heard about something called GEDmatch, a free database where one can upload their DNA results from any of the "big 3" DNA testing companies, thereby widening your search and allowing you to compare with someone who didn't take the same test you did.

We both checked our FTdna results after I tested, hoping for a connection, but didn't find one. Then, late one night here/early in the morning over there, we were chatting on Skype, and I said, "Hey, why don't you run our kit numbers?" She did, and found out we are about 6th cousins!! FTdna doesn't go out as far on their matching results as GEDmatch does! Friends for 20 years turn out to be related!

Now, through an answer to prayer which played out in classic "Six Degrees of Separation" (the theory that we are all separated from everyone else in the world by no more than six people between us), social media played a huge role in the best connection of my life!

I was Facebook friends with one of the students who attended the international boarding school where I taught for a few years. She "introduced" me to an older couple that she knew through a church association. They in turn "introduced" me to a friend of theirs, a genealogist, also here in Oregon. Somewhere along the way, I also became friends with a fellow adoptee named Kim, from a random public adoption-related post. Kim's cousin through adoption is friends with her, and with the genealogist on Facebook, and so was able to see something I posted or commented on specific to adoption that struck a chord with her, so she sent me a friend request. I clicked over to see who her friends were, figured out she was an adoptee, and said, sure, why not?

Almost immediately, this new friend, Raeleah, and I, started comparing notes and joking as adoptees will do (since we really have no idea) that we might be related, because we seemed to have a lot in common. We were both adopted by older childless Seventh-day Adventist couples, raised as only children, went to church schools, drive Cavaliers (hers is red, mine is white) and so on. While that was fun, we just didn't have any idea until we exchanged "kit numbers" (I had Judi in the UK run all of ours). Imagine our shock and delight to learn that not only was I related to Judi, I was related to Raeleah, AND they are both related to each other! They also turned out to be related to several other cousins I already knew or had met on FTdna!

Raeleah and I live about 3 ½ to 4 hours apart here in Oregon, so we began planning a way to meet in the middle, which we did for the first time in March of 2014. It was truly incredible, meeting a total stranger who you feel closer to instantly, than anyone you've ever known in your whole life. We were like two peas in a pod in our interests, mannerisms, taste in food, shopping, interacting with strangers, taking pictures. . .

To demonstrate what kind of impact this has had on my life – I attended church boarding school for the last two years of high school, and each year my school has an alumni homecoming weekend for all who ever attended or worked there. Every year, months ahead of this event, I would get this longing, this feeling in my gut that I had to go back. I never found whatever it was that kept drawing me back there, but I went every chance I could.

This year, after finding Raeleah, that feeling is gone. I had no desire to go back, and I unfriended a large number of former classmates that I was not close to, because of the huge paradigm shift that took place in finding my missing puzzle piece. Even though the DNA currently indicates we are about 6th cousins, we have so much in common, including our overall physical build, our small hands, our taste in foods and hats and music...every time we meet it's another adventure in exploring who we are together. We also sadly share the experience of having birth mothers who want nothing to do with us, and who refuse to disclose who our fathers are, and continue to work and dig and share whatever occurs to us as we pore over our respective DNA results in search of answers.

While my birth mother claimed she had been raped and didn't know who my father was, she had given the doctor who delivered me quite a specific description, which was shared with my adoptive mother, who worked in the same clinic, although they never met. Once I moved to Georgia and met some maternal first cousins back there, one of them and her mother had told me who they thought my father was, based on the description. I have held onto that for years, and have researched his name and family tree at length, but have gotten nowhere definite.

Around 2002, after focusing on where he grew up, I put on my journalist/researcher cap and started calling all the high schools in St. Louis where they might have been students in the 1940s. Thankfully, I didn't get too far down the list before I hit pay dirt, and got in touch with someone with the alumni association who was very helpful. She put me in touch with this man's sister, Carol, who was living in Washington while I was still in Georgia.

Carol shared with me their mother's name, and her mother's maiden name, and I worked on that for about a decade. She told me her brother had been married "at least six times." She told me about his sons —more half-brothers?! I spoke to one of the sons years ago (his father had left their mother while she was pregnant with him and his fraternal twin) but didn't get far. He really didn't want anything to do with me or that side of his family.

Fast forward to living in Oregon, and no longer having a good number for the aunt. Bring in fellow adoptee search angels, and I get a number and address for Carol in no time flat. I called her and explained my need for her to take a DNA test, in order to confirm or rule out her brother as my father. She said she needed to think about it and would get back to me.

Two weeks pass, nothing. I called her back, she said she understands my situation, and with reservation, agreed to the test. The next morning she phoned me and I thought, "Oh no, she's changed her mind." As it turns out, she had not.

No, she just wants me to send a notarized statement, which I did, as follows:

> "This is to certify that no additional requests or requirements will be made of the person providing the DNA sample, to wit, Carol ____, or her immediate family, once the sample has been submitted for testing to Family Tree DNA, the results have been revealed to her, and to the person requesting this test, Dorothy Fletcher."

Being the compliant adoptee, I agree, and to my disgust, I actually hear myself saying, "If you don't want any further contact after we get the results of the test, that's ok. I'm used to that."

I had told her what description I had of my possible birth father (a "tall, blonde-haired blue-eyed German who was known to the family") and she said, "No, Ray had brown hair and hazel eyes." I told her that my DNA results indicated my father was Jewish and she said, "No, we would have known that. We are German and Bohemian." (uh huh...I'm not writing him off yet – of my Jewish matches have those countries in common) She did indicate that she was now curious, so I took that as a good sign.

I wrote the statement, got it notarized at the bank, mailed it off with a return receipt, ordered the test from FTdna and kept checking the tracking like someone waiting for a note from a lover to appear in my inbox! I saw that she got it, but heard nothing, saw nothing on the website (I was given the kit number and a password just like she was) so I dropped her an email, letting her know I had set the privacy settings on there so no one should see it but me and her, and still nothing.

I waited two more days, sent another email and decided I would call if I still didn't hear from her, but she emailed back that she had been out of town, and that she had in fact swabbed her cheek and sent it back the very next day, and signed it, "Blessings, Carol."

Another day passed, I checked the website, and it indicated that the lab has received her kit! Now we wait...to see if Carol's brother was or was not my father. After her cool response, I found myself hoping we are NOT related. I would be disappointed to not even have a name, but it would clear the slate and let me just start over. I just want and need to know, once and for all.

If it turns out he was not my father, then I'm in search of a tall, blonde-haired blue-eyed German who was messing about in Bakersfield, California in May of 1960. Right.

My advice through all of this is never give up, never stop asking for help and support from other adoptees, and never reject any information you get out of hand, as there may be a kernel of truth to it.

I have found some wonderful people through my DNA matches who actually want to know who I am, how we are related, and some have even paid for extra tests on their parents to figure out which one I am related to! The "sister/cousin" I found through the "Six Degrees" was truly an answer to both of our prayers, and while all of the recent discoveries have been rewarding, heart-warming and confidence- building, it was in finding her that I finally feel that I am no longer alone. We now have each other. And if I never find out who my father is (but I intend to!) it has all still been better than nothing.

Who is **Sophi Fletcher**? I'm a work in progress. I'm even trying out a brand new name these days, which makes me more confident and comfortable in my own skin than I have ever been. I'm a God-fearing, praise-singing, road-trip loving, drive-by-shooting photographer, former speech coach and English teacher. I'm an adoptee in recovery, reunion, reinvention and reformation. I will never stop searching for answers to my truth and my whole identity. I am a genealogically-minded, DNA-tested Facebook addict who uses the medium to connect with other adoptees and the cousins I find through DNA testing, and to educate those who need it/are open to it. I enjoy creating Facebook pages for friends and businesses I support, and I'm a purveyor of postcards I make for my little town, which I refer to affectionately as Mayberry.

I'm also a former journalist, presently a part-time writer, editor, proofreader, and a former ESL (English as a Second Language) teacher, who dreams of becoming an online accent reduction and assimilation coach one day. I love art and music, American history, primitive antiques, and thrift shopping. I am always looking for a bargain. This ties in well with my organizational skills (apart from my computer desk!) as I love to rearrange furniture and my "treasures." Last, but certainly not least, I am currently a live-in caregiver to my elderly adoptive mother, and mom to an adorable, yet ornery, diabetic cat.

The Adoptee's Healing Journey
From "Rejected" To Beloved

by Karen Caffrey, LPC, JD

Three days before writing this, my birth grandniece was born on the other side of the country. Although physically separated from her birth by 3000 miles, modern technology has come to the rescue. I and other family members have been participating as much as possible in the events surrounding her birth though Facebook, FaceTime, texts, emails and phone calls. (I sit in my Connecticut living room looking at a Facebook picture of my grandniece asleep in a crib in California, while my sister stands in front of the crib holding an iPad, while FaceTiming with her husband and son in Texas. Cool!)

Everyone is thrilled about the safe arrival of this precious new life and newest member of our family. I can feel a collective sigh of relief across the country that my grandniece and her mother survived delivery, and are healthy, content and well. Everyone is trying on their new identities. My nephew is an uncle. My birth parents are now great grandparents. My sister is a grandmother. She has chosen to be called Nonna; her husband will be Poppa J. We are all eagerly imagining our future together with this beautiful little girl.

Bathing in the reality of such an outpouring of love and welcome towards this infant, I have been struck that my arrival in the world, and that of my fellow adoptees, was almost without exception very, very different. Many of our extended relatives were not even aware of our births. Our mothers (and fathers) were either planning on being separated from us, or were being forced or coerced to do so. Our grandparents were unaware of this impending separation, complicit in it, or were in fact responsible for orchestrating it.

Good God.

This is just the beginning of the story about the circumstances that lead so many adoptees to feeling rejected. There are a plethora of others. These include, but are not limited to, being treated as less than or different from blood relatives by family, friends, teachers and society at large; implicitly or explicitly threatened with abandonment, withdrawal of love or judgment due to one's adopted status or anything connected to it (viz. – interest in one's origins or a desire to search); the stigma of illegitimacy or "bad blood"; lacking physical or racial similarity with one's adoptive family or community; birth parents or other family members refusing contact or a relationship later in life; and/or being legally discriminated against by one's government (viz. – denied access to original birth certificates or adoption court files.) Oh, and I must mention a final, "umbrella" circumstance faced by adoptees, namely denial by the dominant culture that any of the foregoing circumstances exist or matter.

Here's a personal example.

I remember as a college freshman I was one of the top scoring students in my Biology 101 Lecture class, and thus a favorite of our professor Miss W. Our lab assignment for the Thanksgiving holiday was to conduct a genetic test on our family members by asking them to put some saliva on a piece of litmus paper, which only changed color if a person had a specific gene.

As I would be celebrating the holiday with my adoptive family I approached Miss W. and asked what an adopted person should do for the homework since she wouldn't be genetically related to her family. Miss W. said she could use another student's data. Then Miss W. asked me, "Karen, are you adopted?" I answered yes. She paused and replied, "Oh.....I wouldn't have thought that of you." Too humiliated and stunned to ask her what she meant, I simply turned and walked away.

Every one of you has one, or a hundred and one, similar tales to tell. So for the purposes of this survival guide, I'm not going to go into great detail to explain or justify the adoptee's feeling of rejection. If you're an adoptee reading this, you know what I'm talking about.

What I want to talk about is what you can do to heal.

To start I want to talk about rejection, and particularly about the meaning of the word "reject". (I checked the dictionary.) "Reject" can be used either as a verb or a noun. Used as a verb, it means to not accept something, to push it away or rebuff it. In this sense it is an action. Used as a noun, however, to reject means that the "who" or "what" we reject is "rejectable," or not worth keeping.

I think the distinction between using "reject" as a verb or as a noun is critically important when we take up the topic of the adoptee's experience of being rejected. The fact is there are two separate perspectives involved. There is one perspective which looks at the action of the birth mother/father/family as the action of "rejecting" (viz. - not parenting) the adoptee. The second perspective is the adoptee's experience of that fact. The adoptee's pain of "rejection" occurs when the action of rejection is translated in the adoptee's body/mind into the experience that she is a person who is worthy of rejection.

This essential dilemma is faced by adoptees and non-adoptees alike. Our sense of our self, our sense of worthiness and acceptability, is strongly based upon the actions others take towards us. (And in this instance, I am including all forms of communication as "actions," such as words, expressions, touch, behaviors, etc.) How our parents and those closest to us acted towards us, particularly when we were children, had a huge influence in creating our subjective sense of self and self-regard.

We adoptees are particularly at risk regarding the phenomenon of concluding that other's actions towards us reflect our worth, due to the timing and nature of the basic "action" in question. From an infant's perspective there has been a permanent loss of the bodily presence of her mother. There is just no way around this. Even if our mother removed herself from us with a loving intention (which was sometimes, though not always, the case) her intention was irrelevant to our infant selves and perspective.

Evolution primed us to attach to our mother (and vice versa): it is a biological imperative necessary to our survival. The loss of her was a catastrophe. Our infant bodies experienced the resulting pain as a deep, amorphous, preverbal relationship trauma. And the trauma happened before our brains developed the kind of conscious awareness that would have enabled us to have a perspective separate from those around us. (viz.–"That's not about me, that's about her.") This trauma had long lasting effects on the capacity of our bodies and minds to relax, open and receive physical and emotional love.

And as Hamlet would say, "there's the rub." For the problem is rarely that there has been no other love to be had in our lives. Even for those of us who faced abusive childhoods, somewhere along the line somebody treated us lovingly. (It is otherwise almost impossible to survive to adulthood.) And for many others of us there in fact existed one, two or several people (a parent, sibling, teacher, friend, partner, etc.) who has sincerely offered us love.

The problem is that we have a hard time receiving the love that is offered. Having translated the verb of being "rejected" into the noun of being "rejectable," we don't believe we are worthy of it. We can't feel the love, we actively dismiss it or we push it away. We stay closed and shut down, attempting to guard against feeling the pain of past events that we may not even consciously remember.

What's a body to do?

Our adoptee bodies (and in my opinion everybody else's bodies) must first, with some small or large part of the mind, grasp the truth that we are not worthy of rejection. Or to phrase it more positively, the truth that we are acceptable, loveable, worthy, whole and holy.

I am fairly certain that the point of existence is love. Just love. In all its permutations and forms. Receiving it; giving it; expressing it; dwelling in it; savoring it; being it. I believe this is true not only for adoptees but for all sentient beings. Somewhere, somehow, I think a person must grasp this essential truth in order to heal. It can be a little like pulling yourself up by your bootstraps, especially at first. And believe me, I understand how difficult this is when the demons in your head are screaming that you are a worm, that your own mother gave you away, that no one has loved you and no one ever will. I really, really understand.

I also really, really understand that these voices are completely mistaken. And I can say that even though we've never met, may never meet, and I know nothing about you. (Other than that you can read, or at least hear and understand the English language.) How do I know? See the immediately preceding paragraph that begins with, "I am fairly certain…"

You must grab onto this truth tightly and hold on with both hands, and do your best to not let it go. For it is what you must hold on to as you step forward into healing the trauma of feeling all the hurt, rage, despair, and grief that are contained in the experience of feeling rejectable and unworthy.

What does that journey look like? I can tell you what mine has looked like so far. I have spent a great deal of time in nature, and both outdoors and indoors with animals. I have consciously sought (though not always achieved) close, revealing friendships and intimate relationships. I have had several therapists over the years, and as a therapist myself, I have sought out and been guided by many gifted trainers and healers. Most of this therapy and training has been in body-based therapies such as Somatic Experiencing, as so much of my distress has been stored in my body and autonomic nervous system.

I've stepped outside of the ordinary and received healing with dream workers, shamans and curanderas. I've drawn, painted, danced, screamed, sung, cried, laughed and wailed. I've taken risks and cowered in fear. And I've also made serious mistakes and hurt people close to me. I've been judgmental, arrogant, contemptuous and cruel. I've worked hard, hard, hard on trying to forgive those who have hurt me and hard, hard, harder on trying to forgive myself for hurting others. I've prayed and asked others to pray for me. I've given up and tried again. And again. And again. And again.

At some point I realized that I had crested the mountain. I felt more worthy of love than not. That I have in truth become my own beloved. I can't pinpoint exactly in what decade of my life this took place. And the journey certainly is not over. But I've learned that reject is a noun. One that I don't have to define myself by. Because beloved is a noun, too.

I believe this is the essence of the adoptee's journey, and probably of any healing journey. That we must enlarge our perspective enough to not just believe, but to sense in our bodies and our bones, that the actions of others in "rejecting" us do not reflect any truth at all about ourselves.

That the truth, in fact, is that we are loveable. That we can viscerally experience this love inside of ourselves and towards ourselves. And that a natural extension of the love we feel towards ourselves is to experience love towards others.

We have, and must, become our own beloved.

Karen Caffrey, LPC, JD is a psychotherapist, a writer, a reunited adoptee and an attorney. She has a private psychotherapy practice in West Hartford, Connecticut and specializes in counseling adult adoptees, attorneys and all those seeking to live more satisfying and open-hearted lives.

She is a Contributing Author to *Adoption Therapy: Perspectives from Clients and Clinicians on Processing and Healing Post-Adoption Issues.* Karen is also President of Access Connecticut Now, Inc. a grassroots organization dedicated to re-establishing the right of adult adoptees to access their original birth certificates (www.accessconnecticut.org).

You can visit her at www.karencaffrey.com and on Facebook at www.facebook.com/KarenCaffreyCounseling.

PART V: SURVIVAL TOOLS

Genealogy: More than Just Branches on A Tree

by Zack Pasters

I always knew that I was adopted but grew up without any knowledge of my biological foundation. I have been interested in genealogy for as long as I can remember, but it really got started at the age of 7 when my adoptive grandfather passed away and I began asking my dad questions about his family that he could not answer. After several years of asking specific questions, and once it became clear that it wasn't a passing phase, my dad took me to the Ohio Historical Society. It was there that my journey truly began and it would eventually lead to finding my birth parents.

I found my biological mother in July of 2006, but sadly she had died just days before and so my first introduction to her was through her obituary. My biological mother was two months shy of 26 years old when I was born. I came as quite a surprise since she was unaware that she was pregnant. She was nearly 6 feet tall and it was not unusual for her weight to fluctuate up and down according to surviving family members. Only a select number of people in her family knew about me – my grandparents who were divorced, both sets of great grandparents and a cousin, who was like a sister to my mother. Outside of these seven people, no other maternal family members knew of my existence.

My birth father knew nothing about me until the day he was called to sign the adoption paperwork. He was 28 years old and newly married to another woman. When I found him a few months after finding my mother, he declined a reunion, and later his two adult sons, my half-brothers, declined as well. Without a reunion, it was a natural progression for me to research the family trees of my biological parents. In a lot of ways, it was far more healing than simply finding them. It enabled me to see the big picture. I was able to see the progression of the family over several generations. That has always fascinated me both with my adoptive and my biological roots, and with those of my friends.

Over time, I became involved with a network of adoptees online through Myspace and Facebook. I began by searching out the roots of people that I had become comfortable enough with to ask if they wanted me to look into their roots. And from there it snowballed into my friends referring other adoptees to me who wanted me to look for their birth parents or look into the roots of their parents. All my searches are done for free.

I try to do as thorough of a search as is humanly possible by using all the resources that I have at my disposal. This ranges from internet research, to going to a library or historical society to try and tease out more information about a family. I use everything from census information to military documents along with other documents found on www.ancestry.com. I also use newspaper articles and obituaries that I find on www.newspaperarchive.com or www.newspapers.com. Another free website that I use is the Mormon genealogy website, www.familysearch.org, where I can find a large number of birth, marriage and death records. They also have a very good collection of probate records ranging from court documents and cases to wills from the 1800's for most of the 50 states.

One of the very nice, yet frustrating features of ancestry.com is that you can build a family tree. You have to register to build it, but it is free and you don't have to have a subscription to the site. What is so maddening about this feature is that I have found a number of these trees to be unsourced and inaccurate. In this case, I will look at a tree that is not sourced and try to verify it with my own research before adding it to the family trees that I have built.

The various family trees that I build on Ancestry are all sourced. You can attach individual documents found on the site to your tree as sources, or you can manually add sources from outside resources. An integral part of good genealogy is citing your sources. When one does not cite their research it is effectively worthless since people looking at your work will not know where you got your information. Much like footnotes, there is a specific format to citing, basically including "who, what and where" in a prescribed format. Learning to cite your research takes time and practice along with patience.

With any narrative, one will find little known or forgotten facts about a family. These facts can be both good and bad. For instance, I worked on a search for a friend who discovered that she was first cousins with E. B. White. She was thrilled by this revelation since he was one of her favorite authors when she was growing up. In my own personal case, I researched a family story claiming ties to the Hatfields who were involved in the famous West Virginia feud. However, no one was sure of the exact relationship and how it figured into the grand scheme of things.

As it turned out, my third great grandfather was the uncle of the infamous Anderson "Devil Anse" Hatfield. However, my research has shown that my specific Hatfield relatives were not directly involved in the feud with the McCoys. While some might wish to bury this bit of infamous family history, I freely talk about it since I think it is too cool not to be shared.

There is always a risk that you will find a deeply buried family secret such as was the case when I discovered a murder within my birth family, a fact that had been hushed up long enough to be forgotten. Research revealed that my second great aunt had custody of her niece since her mother had died young. The father was still alive and allowed to see her, but she lived with her aunt and uncle. According to the sensational newspaper accounts, on Christmas Eve of 1923, my second great uncles, who were twins, pulled up to the farm of their sister and her husband. The twins accused them of turning the little girl against them, and a heated argument ensued.

Things quickly spiraled out of control and became physical when one of the twins pulled out a revolver firing three bullets, two to the chest and one point blank to the head, of their brother-in-law. The murder took place in the presence of several people including the child, her older sister, and the sister of the murderers. I found this account to be astonishing not only because of the graphic nature of the family tragedy, but also because it led to the discovery that I was a third cousin to the next door neighbors of my adoptive parents before they moved with me to our current home. We have all been astonished by this incredible coincidence.

It gives me a great feeling of satisfaction to use my passion to help other adoptees discover their biological roots. Not only has it helped me in my own journey, it has also enabled me to grow as a person. I've wanted to use my skills professionally for years, but have never had the gumption to follow through. Helping others has given me confidence in my skills and I am preparing to begin the certification process in the near future.

However, I will continue to strive to do searches for adoptees free of charge. I would encourage everyone, regardless if they are adopted or not, to look into their family history. I am inspired by a quote from Marcus Garvey, which sums things up nicely:

> "A people without the knowledge of their past history, origin and culture is like a tree without roots."

I was adopted at 6 weeks of age through Richland County Children's Services. I was born in Ohio and grew up near Columbus, Ohio. I am 37 years old and have had a fascination with history and genealogy for at least 30 of those years. I like to read mostly historical fiction and the classics such as The Idiot by Fyodor Dostoyevsky. I also like to watch TV shows that are well written such as the Walking Dead and Sons of Anarchy – **Zack Pasters**

Finding Answers Through DNA Testing

by Gaye Sherman Tannenbaum

Introduction

Everybody's doing it these days. Amazing stories abound and you may be very tempted to try it yourself. What is stopping you? For many adoptees, it is the fear of disappointment. When you've invested 20+ years in a fruitless search with dead ends and roadblocks everywhere you turn, it's hard to get excited about "the next best thing". Will it really help, or will you just be throwing away more money?

The answer right now, unfortunately, is that "your mileage may vary". The good news is the odds of finding meaningful information will only get better. Trust me on this. I've been doing DNA testing for eight years now. The information I now receive on a daily basis compared to what I received from my first DNA test in 2006 is on the scale of running a brand new Retina Display MacBook Pro versus a Commodore 64. It's the DeLorean from 'Back to the Future' versus a Model T. A Boeing 777 versus the Wright Brothers at Kitty Hawk. Seriously. Pull up a comfy chair and have a look.

This isn't your grandparents' DNA testing

DNA testing. Brings up images of CSI or at least Maury Povich. Blood tests. Paternity tests. Crime scene evidence. FBI databases. Very expensive stuff. Is that what we're talking about? No, not at all.

Modern DNA testing is done using cheek cells. Some tests use a simple scrubbing from the inside of your mouth. Other tests use saliva. Just spit into the tube, cap it, and mail it to the lab – all from the comfort of your own home. Tests generally run about $99 and there IS a price war going on.

Relatively painless science refresher

Your DNA contains the blueprint for creating you. It is the accumulation and mixture of DNA from your distant ancestors. You may be familiar with the 23 pairs of chromosomes that make up human DNA. These chromosomes are contained in the nucleus of each of your cells. There are twenty-two pairs numbered 1 through 22 (the autosomes), plus the X and Y chromosomes (the sex chromosomes). You get one of each chromosome from your mother and one from your father. Females have two X chromosomes and males have one X and one Y chromosome. Males receive the X chromosome from their mothers and the Y chromosome from their fathers. Mitochondrial DNA is also in each cell but not contained in the nucleus. Mitochondrial DNA (mtDNA) is passed from mother to child.

Available tests and what they can tell you

Modern DNA tests compare your DNA to that of others taking the same test with the same company (the company's database) and to researched populations.

mtDNA – Available from Family Tree DNA. This kind of DNA is passed intact from mother to child. The picture it contains is from your mother's mother's mother's mother's mother's mother – your strict maternal line. It is useful for determining ethnic background. Just remember that this is only ONE line in your ancestry. If your strict maternal line 8th great grandmother was the proverbial "Indian princess" your mtDNA would show Native American origins even if no other ancestors were of Native American origin.

Y-DNA – Available from Family Tree DNA and for males only as the Y chromosome is only passed from father to son. The picture it contains is from a male's father's father's father's father's father's father – the strict paternal line. If you are female, your son's Y-DNA comes from HIS father's line and has no connection to YOUR paternal line. Like mtDNA, it is useful in determining the ethnic background of your strict paternal line. There is an additional advantage. Surnames are generally passed from father to son along with the Y chromosome. This means that males taking a Y-DNA test MAY learn their father's surname.

Autosomal DNA – Available from Family Tree DNA, 23andMe, and Ancestry.com. This is the test we had all been waiting for and it was first offered by 23andMe in 2009 at the introductory price of $499. All three companies are now selling the same test with MORE features for $99. This test will give you "ethnic admixture" (the 1/4 German, 1/2 Irish stuff) and give you a list of people in their database whose DNA matches yours (your genetic cousins).

Excited yet?

So what do I get for my money?

Ethnic origins: Each of the three companies has its own way of measuring ethnic admixture. This has come a LONG way from 23andMe's initial stab at it. Back in 2011, I was told I was "100% European". Can we say "Big Whoop-Dee-Doo"? Since then, each company has completely or partially overhauled their admixture predictions and they continue to do so – at no further cost to those purchasing a test.

My latest results:

23andMe	Ancestry.com	Family Tree DNA
47.6% Ashkenazi	43% European Jewish	44% Jewish Diaspora
34.5% British & Irish	14% Great Britain	
	7% Ireland	
5.6% French & German	20% Europe West	15% Western/Central Europe
5.5% Broadly Northern European	9% Scandinavia	17% Scandinavia
	1% Finland/Northwest Russia	6% Finland and Northern Siberia
1.4% Italian	<1% Italy/Greece	
1.7% Broadly Southern European	5% Iberian Peninsula	18% Southern Europe
3.6% Broadly European		
0.1% Unassigned		

Getting better but obviously not an exact science. Ancestry.com initially had an overabundance of "Scandinavian" in their predictions. Quite a few people complained so they went back to the drawing board. Family Tree DNA rolled out their new predictions last year. Expect more changes every year or so.

One problem is when to "stop the clock". The Vikings repeatedly invaded the British Isles throughout history, so lots of Britons who can trace their family back 500 years won't count the Viking ancestors who arrived in 1100. The DNA is still there but should we call it "Scandinavian" or "British"? You see the problem.

Cousin matching: A number cruncher's dream come true. Are you hoping you'll be matched with a dozen or so people in the database? Think again. You will see hundreds, if not thousands, of genetic cousins. Yes, you are genetically related to all…those…people. For adoptees whose only known genetic relatives are the ones we gave birth to, this is heady stuff.

That's the good news. The bad news is that 85% of these genetic cousins are going to be pretty distant – common ancestors back around 1700 or earlier. This used to frustrate people with meticulously researched 10 generation trees who matched others with similarly detailed genealogies. "How come we can't find our common ancestor?" It's quite different now.

Over the years, two things have happened: More people have tested and participants have learned (mostly from each other) how to best analyze their results. As a result, many more people are able to find their common ancestors using DNA testing and some have used it to break through a brick wall or two. Good news for adoptees and donor-conceived and anyone else with a big gaping hole in their family tree.

Can you get matched with a first cousin, a sibling or even a parent? As recently as two years ago, getting a bona fide second cousin match was "hitting the DNA lottery". I had predicted that in five years' time, second cousin matches would become more common. I'm happy to say that I was wrong. It is happening now. People are getting matched with second cousins on a regular basis. My current husband (not adopted) has been matched with three second cousins, four second cousins once removed, three third cousins and a host of others I have been able to link to his tree. Two years ago, he had ONE - a 5th cousin once removed.

Eight years after my first DNA test, I got my first second cousin match on my unknown paternal side. Miracles happen even for me. For my kids – not so much. I have yet to see a useful match on their father's side. Still, hope springs eternal.

So why the difference? Remember "your mileage may vary"? Part of that is pure luck - you have a second cousin out there who has tested. Mostly, it is ethnicity. The best odds are for those of US colonial ancestry. What tips the odds in your favor:

- Ancestors are not "recent" (post 1850) immigrants.
- Availability of records and researched genealogies.
- Current generations are interested in genealogy.
- Current generations are interested in, and have ready access to, DNA testing.

Endogamous populations (Ashkenazi Jewish, French Canadian, Mennonites) are a two-edged sword. You will get more matches on average, due to the same DNA being "recycled" over and over, but it will be difficult to untangle the spaghetti. I'm currently working on a father search where the adoptee was matched with several people who descended from various combinations of marriages between six families in the same area of Alabama.

You've got some pretty smart cousins

In addition to the three main companies offering DNA testing, there are legions of people who have not only purchased the available DNA tests for themselves and a few dozen relatives, they are actively creating tools for analyzing the results. Many of them are freely sharing their tools with anyone who wants to use them. Others are volunteering their expertise to help newbies understand their DNA results. Veteran search angels are learning how to use DNA testing. This aspect of the DNA testing community has exploded in the past two years.

Third-Party Tools

Independent researchers and "citizen scientists" are constantly developing new applications and methodologies for public use. Some, like triangulation and admixture analysis, are being used by the general public.

Others, such as chromosome mapping and persistent segment analysis, are still being investigated and do not as yet have any "user-friendly" computer applications associated with them.

One of the key methods helping adoptees identify close and immediate family is called triangulation. Triangulation is the analysis of matches in common; the matches that any two or more people share with one another. The idea is that three or more people who are all genetic matches to each other likely share a limited number of common ancestors. Find the common ancestors for group of matches who are all matches to you and to each other AND who share more or less the same DNA segment and you have just identified some of your ancestors.

They may be your 5th great grandparents but once you repeat the exercise with other groups of common matches and identify more of your distant ancestors, the next step is to look for the next generation down – where a descendant from the common ancestors in one group married a descendant from the common ancestors in another group. In other words – you have identified John Collins and Abigail Richmond as your 5th great grandparents and you have also identified James Bradford and Olivia Hayes as another set of 5th great grandparents. When you build out your family tree, you may find a grandson of John and Abigail who married a granddaughter of James and Olivia. Congratulations! You may have just identified your 3rd great grandparents.

Sounds like a lot of work

Yes it is. Remember those smart cousins? Producing groups of matches in common and matches who share common segments used to be extremely tedious, even with the use of spreadsheets. The Autosomal DNA Segment Analyzer (ADSA) from DNAGedcom.com uses your Family Tree DNA match and segment data to produce a handy report that combines shared segments with matches in common. The result is a clear picture of groups of your matches who very likely all share a common ancestor.

Simplified Portion of ADSA Triangulation Report

Match Name	Chr	Start	End	cM	SNPs	ICW	Segments
A	4	99784875	111846805	10.84	2500		
B	4	99784875	118613059	16.28	3800		
C	4	101870440	118613059	14.06	3200		
D	4	155924594	165482105	9.88	2000		
E	4	155924594	166234215	10.68	2200		
F	4	155924594	166234215	10.68	2200		
G	4	179572255	183968731	9.88	1543		
H	4	179784531	187316378	17.80	2497		
I	4	183071122	187798792	12.92	1597		
J	4	183071122	187798792	12.92	1597		

An ADSA report contains the match's name and email address (shown above as A through J) and shared segment information (chromosome, start and end location, and segment length in centiMorgans).

This is just one of many tools out there with more on the horizon.

It's a pretty steep learning curve and luckily there are many people who will guide you, review your results and make recommendations. If you have a working knowledge of Excel or are decently computer savvy, you can do a lot of the work yourself. Volunteers can only handle so many cases at one time, especially if they are doing all the work.

It's going to be an adventure for sure. You will definitely learn a lot about your ancestry and will more than likely find your immediate family – but it won't necessarily happen overnight. The good news is, you can be totally hands off and just wait for that second cousin match to find you!

Gaye Sherman Tannenbaum is a retired forensic accountant, currently living in Uruguay. She is a New York adoptee who reunited with her mother about five years ago and now spends her time as a DNA search angel and access restoration advocate. A Late Discovery Adoptee, she was finally told "the big secret that everyone knew" in 1984, at age 31 and credits her online adoptee and first mom friends for keeping her sane during her journey. When she's not paying it forward by doing searches and advising others, she can usually be found commenting on adoptee rights, DNA and genealogy throughout the Internet.

Searching is My New Normal

by Lynn Grubb

"Maybe you are searching among the branches,
for what only appears in the roots." – Rumi

It's been about ten years now since I went from a non-searcher to a searcher that winter day when I logged into Adoption.com to read this important bit of information posted in an adoptee forum:

"For those of you adopted in Illinois, your real birth name is on your final adoption documents."

I didn't know the person who posted it, but I want to thank them from the bottom of my heart. This was the moment when the light bulb turned on. I immediately started digging through a box of records to locate the adoption petition and decree I had in my possession for years. There it was:

Baby Girl Unger

It was not a nickname as I had been told. It was the first piece of my identity. I was of German ancestry. This came as a surprise as I had never identified with being German, even though the community I was a member of growing up, was full of Germans. Other than bratwursts, I couldn't think of any German food that I actually liked. In my heart, I wanted to be Italian.

I had been told by my adoption agency (via the non-identifying information) that my father's people were thought to be Italian-born. I love Italian food so much that I worked in Italian restaurants for more than a decade of my adult life. People tell me I look Italian. For twenty years, I embraced the food, the culture and the identity of being Italian.

Shortly after I located my maternal birth family, and verified my German heritage, a genealogist friend created my maternal tree on Ancestry.com. Staring at the empty branches of my pedigree always gave me pause. I longed to know about the other half of my family. Was I more like them than the maternal family I struggled to identify with?

I decided to take a genetic DNA test to provide more information on my father's ancestors. The Family Tree DNA, Family Finder Autosomal DNA test, was my first choice. I had reached a dead-end with learning who my father was and realized that if I was ever going to find the other half of my ancestry, genetic genealogy was going to lead the way. I had tried my best to get paternal information from my birth mother; however, she insisted that she just didn't know anything about my father except that he was possibly Mexican or Spanish and "wasn't from here".

When my results at Family Tree DNA in March of 2013 were posted, I was elated. The first screen I clicked into was Population Finder (now called myOrigins) to see my ethnic breakdown. I scanned through each category and noticed that Italian was not part of my ethnic makeup according to Family Tree DNA. I was deflated learning this.

Not too long after my results were posted and my DNA matches determined, I was introduced to a distant cousin who was something of a DNA guru. He helped me to make more sense of my ethnic ancestry results. He advised that I was no Italian – with such a large percentage of Native American and other clues – he was certain that I was Hispanic (both Spanish and Latin American) on my father's side.

This was shocking information to take in. Being very light-skinned, the Native American piece was a complete surprise. Talk about an identity shift! Between having to re-write my history in my mind and heart, I had to digest that almost everything written about my father in the adoption agency records was potentially false.

The good news was that my newfound cousin/DNA guru became my search angel and proceeded to amass large amounts of information for me in the town where I was conceived, as he was a local. I am forever indebted to him for his kindness in reaching out to a genetic stranger.

With no close matches at Family Tree DNA, I decided to test with 23 and Me ("to fish in more ponds"). At the time I tested with this company, they were still offering medical DNA results (the FDA has since halted this). Living for four decades with no medical history had left me scared to actually know what inherited diseases could be lurking in my genetic code. Prior to testing with this company, I had been ascribing to the thought, "I really don't want to know" however, I was scared enough over the years to be vigilant in getting pap smears and mammograms, beginning earlier ("just in case") and testing more often than generally recommended to most women with a family history.

Besides learning during reunion that my deceased maternal grandmother had breast cancer late in life, my living maternal uncle had survived colon cancer, and my mother had varicose veins, I had received very little helpful medical history from my maternal side, even in reunion. However, I did learn my mother was born with a rare condition (a hole in her heart) for which she underwent life-saving surgery. This important medical information never made it into my adoption file nor were medical updates ever sought by my adoption agency. (contrary to what opponents of open records claim, family medical history is vitally important in preventing and detecting medical conditions and is sorely lacking for anyone adopted during the Baby Scoop Era).

23 and Me gave results for markers for the big genetic diseases: Parkinson's, Breast Cancer, Ovarian Cancer and Alzheimer's. You had to unlock your results before 23 and Me would allow you to see if you were positive or negative for the marker, as I imagine the company recognized some people may not want to know. I unlocked my results for all of the diseases except Alzheimer's. I was too scared and it took me another six months to be able to open it. I learned I was negative for all of the markers.

Still hoping for a close DNA match to my father, I recently decided to take Ancestry's autosomal DNA test. In addition, I asked my adult biological son to test with 23 and Me to further our chances of getting a DNA match on my paternal side. My results at Ancestry have been very revealing and have again confirmed my Native American roots. One of the features I like about Ancestry DNA is that I can view many of my DNA matches' family trees and Ancestry's software tells you which surnames you share with your DNA matches, making the process of finding your common ancestor much easier.

As for my unknown paternal side, in all three DNA databases, I see multiple Spanish surnames (i.e. Cruz, Perez, Sanchez, etc.) repeating in my cousin matches. These cousins are somehow related to my biological father's side of the family. I await a close match with a first or second cousin to finally fill the missing branches of my tree.

There are some evenings when a friend of mine and I spend hours sifting through surnames of DNA cousins and studying where the cousins' live, what surnames my cousins share and look for ways to connect the dots to my paternal line. In the process, I have become a huge enthusiast of genetic genealogy. I am currently in the process of educating myself by reading blogs and taking part in DNA/genetic genealogy Facebook groups in an effort to learn as much as I can to help myself and others. I also enjoy showing others my DNA results to encourage more interest and participation amongst people I know on-line and in real life.

However, the mystery of my paternal side remains. I have recently become bolder in my outreach for information and have posted in several private Facebook rooms with my story. The reactions have varied from people feeling sorry for me, to people cheering for me, to people shaming me for "not having a good enough relationship with my mother so that she would tell me the truth". Several complete strangers have recently offered to help me in my search as they feel a personal connection to my story. One thing I have learned is that trying to dig up bones more than four decades later is challenging yet, so interesting. I marvel at how many amazing people I have met along this journey.

The last ten years, I have been searching continuously when time allows. It is truly my new normal. This searching has touched the lives of my family members, my friends and the adoption community as a whole, as we share our emotional journeys, our searching methods, and tips on how to maneuver within the still-closed adoption system and these amazing, growing genetic genealogy websites.

I am a believer that my own searching spreads hope to other non-searchers who may think that their birth families are not interested in them or that their ancestry and medical history don't matter. These things matter a lot to almost everybody, and adoptees are not exempt from their desire to know more about the people and places that resulted in their existence.

One of the many positive outcomes of my DNA testing and searching that I did not anticipate before I began this journey, was the many new friendships I have made – some blood related and some not. No matter what you ultimately find during your search, you will discover, as I have, that, searching brings the community of adoptees together in a shared, common goal.

Searching may even change how you see yourself. I feel braver, stronger and more complete than ever before.

Survival tips:

1. Give yourself permission to seek answers to your questions, regardless of what those around you say.

2. Seek out a support group, search angels, and genealogists, and use the resources at your library.

3. Don't be afraid to put your story out on social media. Many families have been found this way.

4. As you get information on your family, build your family tree at Ancestry. This pedigree will be invaluable to you if you decide to take the plunge into DNA testing.

5. If you have special investigative skills or knowledge about genetic genealogy, offer this help to others in the adoption community.

Lynn Grubb is an Illinois adoptee, stepmother, biological mother and adoptive parent. She is a contributing author to Lost Daughters and to various adoption anthologies including the newly released, *Dear Wonderful You: Letters to Adopted & Fostered Youth.*

Lynn's first attempt at publicly writing about adoption was during a free poetry class offered at her public library. When the teacher read her poem about adoption, she became visibly upset and shaken by its contents. Lynn didn't give up writing about adoption and found others like her who feel compelled to write about the complexities of being adopted.

Besides writing, Lynn also enjoys singing, playing the violin and the keyboard, and watching true crime shows, which sparked her interest in DNA and genetic genealogy. Two years ago, Lynn began blogging about her DNA discoveries at her blog, No Apologies for Being Me. More recently, she became active in adoptee rights with The Adoptee Rights Coalition and is a volunteer co-facilitator of the Adoption Network Cleveland (Miami Valley) general discussion group.

After having a "Eureka" moment at church one day, she envisioned The Adoptee Survival Guide helping adoptees everywhere.

Lynn lives with her husband and two children in Dayton, Ohio.

Taking the Clock Out of Your Recovery Process

by Deanna Doss Shrodes

Being the one to adjust has always seemed to be at the top of my adoptee job description. Going at the pace of others instead of my own natural pace seemed to be a requirement whenever I hit a bump in the road. Finally at 47 years old, a boundary was erected – by me, and reinforced by my therapist, Melissa Richards.

After experiencing a major falling out with my natural mother, I immediately pursued professional help to give me insight and strength to move forward.

After explaining that what I had encountered throughout my life was complex trauma, Melissa gave me my assignment. I was to do absolutely nothing but grieve – for as long as it took. I was instructed not to rush, but to be sad for as long as it took, and move through the stages of grief. Skipping a stage was sure to impede my healing.

"Sit in this and be sad. Give yourself permission to feel it," she said.

It was time for me to move beyond the old habits of detaching and responding with means that were destructive. For years, in response to the trauma I faced my response was workaholism, perfectionism, emotional and binge eating, among others.

In therapy I came to realize the many beliefs I held that affected me in not healing from the past. The first was an adjustment I needed to make in the way I viewed the forgiveness and reconciliation process as it relates to trauma. As not only a Christian but a minister of 27 years, I had always thought that it was unhealthy, not to mention unbiblical, to not get over anything that happens to you, immediately. It was the whole, "Don't let the sun go down on your wrath" biblical principle. I discovered that dealing with wrath is different than recovering from complex trauma. I wasn't after revenge, I just wanted relief.

I personally believe there are three stages of forgiveness: the will to forgive, the process of forgiveness, and then the state of forgiveness. You decide to forgive someone as an act of your will. Then you go through a process in your heart of working through things, and then finally you come to the point of living in the state of forgiveness. God has helped me go through that process so many times.

This time, I struggled with guilt that the process was taking more time, primarily because it had to do with my mother. Though I willed in my heart to forgive her even in the midst of the painful conversation, and even after receiving the two painful letters, the process was taking time. I was not emotionally ready to reach out again, for a while. And I had no idea when I'd be ready.

Melissa explained to me, I was still actively in-process – moving toward healing and forgiveness, but it was going to take time. The deeper traumas are, the more time it takes to move forward. In my case I was moving forward, not only from the most recent situation with my mother, but also from other unresolved issues connected to my adoption.

There were moments I felt horrible that it was taking a significant amount of time. I would come to realize what I was dealing with was guilt, which is not of God. Conviction of the Holy Spirit moves us to make changes God wants us to make, but guilt doesn't come from Him. I would just imagine myself reaching out to call her number or writing a letter, and I would dissolve to a pile of tears. I felt guilty for feeling that way, though I couldn't identify the reason for the guilt except that taking time to talk to somebody again, especially my mother, just didn't feel right. I learned that much of the grace I extended to others, I didn't give to myself. That needed to change.

"You're just not ready," Melissa would say. "And that's okay. Can I invite you to take the time clock out of this process and allow yourself to take as much time as it takes to recover?"

I took comfort in the fact that in scripture, all were not healed instantly. Some were, as scripture says, "Healed as they went."

Through Melissa's gentle guidance I came to realize the importance of respecting the process and not skipping over any steps that God had for me to take on my journey of healing.

My therapist encouraged me to take all the time in the world to heal, but more than one person indicated they expected me to just snap out of it and move on.

Several times, my sister who is a Christian also, expressed strong disagreement with the process taking time. She wanted it to be quickly resolved and felt like this was the only proper spiritual response. Surely Jesus would not want me to take so much time before reaching out again to my mother. I shared that I was in counseling and to recover properly it had to be at the pace I could handle, not the one that others expected of me.

I also shared with her that I had written our mother a six-page letter pouring my heart out and said everything I had to say. I had nothing more to say to her at the time, and all that was left for me to do right now was heal. I even said, "God forbid if something were to happen to her tomorrow, I've said all that I need to say and have done it in a loving manner."

We agreed to disagree.

In the fourth month of therapy, I was feeling stronger daily, yet still working through the anger stage of grief.

One morning I was taking my two dogs out to walk and I felt so guilty that I was almost four months out and still processing so much and not at the point where I could handle picking up the phone. I literally said aloud, "God, are you truly okay with this?"

I'm sure if somebody was walking by and overheard, they may have thought, "Yeah lady...God is okay with you walking two dogs..."

Mother's Day came and I was emotionally unable to call. I knew in my heart I would be set back in my progress in therapy, if my mother went on the attack in our conversation. So, I sent a card.

Sitting in our session the next week I said, "Melissa, I've gotten some pressure to resolve this quicker and aside from external pressure from others, I'm feeling internal pressure."

Once more, she identified it as guilt.

"Deanna, we're going to practice listening prayer right now. We're both going to pray, in silence. You're going to ask God, 'How long is okay? How long is acceptable for this to last?' And while you're praying, I'm going to pray for you."

We both closed our eyes and silently prayed.

As we did, I sensed God saying, "As long as it takes, Deanna. As long as it takes."

When I opened my eyes, Melissa said, "Did you hear anything from the Lord?"

"Yes, I did. He said let it take as long as it takes," I said.

"Okay," she said, "then let's do that."

In a stunning twist of events, just a week later, my sister and step father called to let me know that my mother had been diagnosed with cancer. They both wanted me to call her immediately. I was in shock and sadness at her diagnosis, but still wasn't ready to call. I took 24 hours to process the information and had an appointment with Melissa to decide what to do.

Through prayer and counsel, I decided that since my mother's condition was so serious, I would interrupt my recovery process temporarily, and contact her. I knew I would regret not making an attempt, if she were to pass away.

I realized that in interrupting the process I was more than likely going to get hurt again and have another mess for Melissa to help me clean up. She told me she would be right there when I got back, to pick up the pieces. And she was.

One thing I felt it was important for anyone connected closely to me to know was that although I was interrupting the process – it was just a temporary pause. No matter what happened, I would be going back to therapy and the same process once my mother was healed, or passed away. At the time several people spoke words that indicated they understood but I knew in my heart when I went right back to my process, it would not be understood.

I was right.

I made the move to contact my mother and it did not go well. In our last conversation, among other things she let me know that she, "did not want her adult-life to start with me," and that she could not accept me as I was.

It was one of the most painful conversations of my life and it was the last I would have with her while she was still coherent enough to talk. My response to her after her saying all those things to me during a 45 minute conversation where I spoke approximately five minutes was: "I only called you for two reasons today. To tell you I'm sorry you have cancer. And to tell you I love you. I'm sorry it's turned into something other than that."
She died eight weeks after she was diagnosed with cancer.

True to my word, I went right back to the recovery process, in therapy.

And, the people I expected to be unhappy about that were indeed unhappy.

I am not sure whether they thought her death should have brought the closure necessary, or that we had all already been through enough without me continuing my former process.

One person mentioned, "She's dead. You're still alive. Just be grateful." (There's that "grateful" word again!)

Perhaps the most powerful thing I learned in therapy was the importance of developing healthy boundaries and keeping them no matter the pressure.

I've learned that people do not view complex trauma, significant loss and complicated grief as other challenges in life. If you are healing from open heart surgery or a car wreck you will receive much greater compassion, for sure.

I try to not live with regrets but one I do have is not creating a boundary sooner and doing what I needed to do, for as long as I needed to do it, to heal.

I am not sure why non-adoptees have such discomfort with our journey through the stages of grief not operating on their time clock. Other than the fact that grief isn't fun for anybody, even the observers. We experience losses throughout our life, and sometimes they are connected to our adoption.

Going forward I've learned to throw away the clock and let people know I'll be walking out the journey on my own terms and at my pace. Anyone who really loves me will understand. And if they don't, I never really had their love or support to begin with. This is a hard reality to accept, yet the same process of grief and recovery will bring the healing needed if I lose them from my life as a result of insisting on taking necessary steps to move forward.

The process is worth it, for me and for all those I love. The best gift I can give them is a healthy and whole, me.

Deanna Doss Shrodes is an Assemblies of God minister, serving for twenty-seven years in pastoral ministry. Currently she serves as the Director of Women's Ministries for the PenFlorida District of the Assemblies of God and is an in-demand speaker in the United States and abroad.

In the adoption community, Deanna is best known for her blog, Adoptee Restoration. An award-winning writer, she is the author of the books *JUGGLE, Manage Your Time...Change Your Life!* and *Worthy to Be Found*. She is a contributing author to five highly acclaimed adoption anthologies, contributing author to *Chocolate for a Woman's Courage*, and a feature writer in scores of publications worldwide, including The Huffington Post.

Deanna and her husband Larry make their home in the Tampa Bay area with their three children.

Finding My Friends

by Cathy Heslin

All my life, I found that I was drawn to other adoptees. Most of the time I didn't know they were adopted when we first became friends. We would discover that we were both adopted and remark on what a coincidence it was.

As I got older, I began to wonder if it was less coincidence and more instinct. Maybe we're drawn to each other for a reason, I pondered.

One of these friends, (I'll call her Carrie), became an anchor for me as I sailed and plummeted the emotions surrounding reunion. Carrie was new into her reunion and I was six years into mine when she asked if I wanted to join her in a support group for adoptees in reunion.

My first thought was, "How is it possible that there are enough adoptees in reunion in this city to have a support group?"

My second thought was, "Hell no!"

The truth was that the thought of doing any more "work" around reunion gave me stomach cramps. I'd been through counseling after I'd first met my birth mother when I was eighteen, and even attended therapy with her four years into our reunion when, after I moved to the town she lived in, I proceeded to pull away from her.

"I'm done with adoption," I told Carrie. "Thanks, but I'm good. I've dealt with it all already."

If only that could be true.

Carrie eventually convinced me to go on the pretense that I could be the "voice of experience" for the group.

That first night, there was a charge just sitting in the room with other adoptees. There were six of us. There were two other women aside from me and Carrie – one who was struggling with a birth mother who didn't want anything to do with her, and another who was a year or two into a "successful" reunion with both parents, but was going through intense internal turmoil that she couldn't explain. There was one guy, who I'll call Tommy. He was more experienced in the stages involved in reunion and had been in therapy for a while.

We each went around and told our stories of adoption and reunion. I explained that I was in reunion with my birth mother but hadn't found my birth father, and that I didn't even know if I wanted to search. "After all, it was hard enough with my birth mother." When I was about to explain why it had been hard with my birth mother, I looked up to see the others nodding at what I was saying.

I couldn't help but laugh. "I'm sorry," I said. "It's just strange to me to not have to explain myself."

"We can talk in shorthand," Tommy said. "You don't have to go into all the details that you would with people on the outside."

It was the first time that being an adoptee meant that I was on the inside of something.

Being part of that group changed me. Before being in that group, I felt crazy for what I was going through. It wasn't part of what we were told as adoptees. We were told that we were lucky, that we were chosen, that it didn't matter that we were adopted. And so whenever we felt otherwise, we felt ostracized. It didn't fit.

But I found a place I fit in. I had a new world with others who were going through similar experiences, where we could talk in shorthand, and where I felt understood in a way I'd never felt before. From that group I went on to find organizations that examined adoption and reunion, and I began to realize there was a whole community of people, much bigger than I'd ever imagined, who were all wrestling, questioning and evolving on adoption and reunion.

My life hasn't been the same since.

I started to realize that maybe that's what I'd been doing on my own as a child when I would find friends who also just happened to be adoptees. Maybe there was something in our shared experience that I recognized, that drew me to them. I was looking for someone who could understand me like no one else.

I don't know if I would have survived the struggle of identity that is part of reunion without the help of my friends. But, not just any friends. The people I relied on – more than friends that I had known since childhood, more than my maid of honor, more than even my husband – are my fellow adoptees.

***

Maybe the best way to explain what it's like, is to give examples of conversations and things I hear from non-adoptees vs. adoptees.

When I discuss my adoption and reunion with non-adoptees, these are the kinds of things I hear:

NON-ADOPTEES

- You're lucky to be adopted, it means your parents really wanted you.

- How wonderful that you have such a big family now that you're in reunion.

- It all worked out for the best.

But, when I have similar conversations with fellow adoptees, the tone is radically different:

ADOPTEES

- I'm so sorry you have to take that on.

- You'll be seeing your whole family? Wow, that's a lot to deal with.

- I know what you're going through.

It's not that my non-adopted friends don't mean well, it's just that they don't understand. We were all raised in a society where clichés about adoption were fed to us as truth.

NON-ADOPTEES

- Your birth mother gave you up because she wanted what was best for you.

- Being adopted is no different than if you were your parents' flesh and blood.

- You're lucky to be adopted. After all, what would have happened to you if your parents hadn't adopted you?

Here are some of the things that I hear in discussions with adoptees that are off from the mainstream understanding, but that resonate with me:

ADOPTEES

- Your birth mother gave you up because she didn't have the resources or support to raise you.

- Being adopted into a family that is not your flesh and blood means you're in a constant struggle to fit in.

- Adoption is actually a money-driven industry where babies are a highly sought-after commodity that are in demand.

I am still learning and growing from my fellow adoptees. Exploring my adoption and reunion experience isn't over. I'm not done. Though sometimes I wish I could be. I write about adoption and reunion and discuss it with others, now with the benefit of the internet through blogs and groups. I'm still learning. I'm still discovering new things about myself. And I still love being understood so fully.

We need each other's stories to be able to understand our own.

Cathy Heslin is a reunited adult adoptee of closed domestic adoption in New Jersey. She currently lives in Portland, Oregon with her husband and two boys. She met her birth mother when she was just 18 and moved out to Portland after graduating college to live with her birth mother. She has been in reunion with her birth mother for nearly 25 years, and with her birth father for 15 and has a complicated extended family that includes all sides of the triad.

She has been writing about adoption for the past five years with a focus on long-term reunion. In addition to writing for Lost Daughters, she has been published in Adoption Constellation magazine. She has written a memoir in partnership with her birth mother called *Kathleen-Cathleen – A True Story of Adoption and Reunion*, where she and her birth mother write alternating chapters sharing their experience of reunion from both the perspective of the adoptee and the birth mother (not yet published). Cathy's personal adoption blog is reunioneyes.blogspot.com. Follow Cathy on Twitter @CathyHeslin.

AFTERWORD

The Last Word: Whose Guide is this Anyway?

by Amanda H.L. Transue-Woolston, MSS, LSW

There's an important question to ask when reflecting and using this book: Whose guide is this anyway?

Those who serve, support, and love adoptees, I want you to know that it's okay not to understand or identify with everything you read in this book, that it's completely normal that adoptees voiced some concepts that were confusing or difficult for you to metabolize. Adoptees, I want you to know that it's okay to write just for you. It's okay to write something that requires the lens of an adopted person to truly understand and to digest. What you write has value even if it doesn't contain mental health advice, reunion insight, or parenting tips others find useful. Other adoptees find your perspective useful. The Adoptee Survival Guide truly is your guide.

As an adult adoptee's role in adoption began in childhood, it is often difficult for others to imagine us as anything other than children when adoption is discussed. We are treated like children in that it's commonplace for our narratives to be shared on public media platforms by everyone but us. Parents, professionals, researchers, and journalists explain our stories, our needs, and our wants – disclosing deeply personal details of our existence, including our images and photographs – from perspectives very different from ours but serving as a substitute for ours nonetheless. It is accepted practice for these discussions to take place, to represent what the experience of being adopted is, without adopted adults being included in the conversation – an adoption conversation without adoptees. We find ourselves asking an important question: Whose story is this anyway?

Adoption policies, as well as social perceptions of adoption, have been formed in large part without us. If we were listened to as we should be, we would not see adoptees deported because federal policy granting citizenship to inter-country adoptees did not cover all adoptees who need citizenship or the safety and identity of children continually disregarded via the amending and sealing of identifying records.

Those we interact with forget we have our own individual, complex experiences in adoption, along with the unique insight those experiences bring. Adoption today is still largely an adoption without adoptees. After years of debating legislators about privacy, ethics, and reproductive justice issues at the intersection of adoptees accessing their original birth certificates, I have begun asking another question: Whose birth was it anyway?

We adoptees are often absent as well in our own writing as far as social perceptions are concerned. Non-adopted members of the adoption constellation and those without a direct connection to adoption alike tend to comb through our writing searching for information they might deem useful. Original parents might look for advice on boundaries in reunion or open adoption. Adoptive parents might look for parenting tips. Professionals serving adoptees (myself included) might look at practice implications. This is always well intentioned and it is indeed wonderful when adoptees are recognized as the go-to sources on what life as an adoptee is like. This is how it should be. What is not wonderful, however, is when our writing is approached exclusively as a teaching tool for those who lack the "adoptee lens" – a unique viewpoint exclusive to those who have the common experiences adoptees share.

If our voices serve only to meet the information needs of others, only others can determine if our voices have value. In reality, when you do not have an "adoptee lens," you cannot comprehensively and fairly appraise the value of an adoptee voice.

My parents are wonderful people who shared their perception with me on what it meant to have adopted a child into their family. Yet, because I didn't have close access to other adopted people to hear their perceptions, my own thoughts about being adopted were underdeveloped as I emerged into young adulthood. I saw adoption as an adoptive parent's experience. I heard my role in adoption explained by my social and religious communities: saved, unwanted, chosen, almost-aborted, lucky, a gift for infertile couples who deserve a child, we're all adopted by God. The strong voice of adopted people is not at the center of how society holds us. Thus, I once viewed adoption without me in it. Now I ask, whose experience is this anyway?

As an adult, I work for a societal and political understanding of an adoption with adoptees present. I work for an adoption with adoptees visible and acknowledged as stakeholders in the adoption community. I work for an adoption culture where adoptees can see themselves in adoption and feel empowered to speak about their experiences, through their art and writing, their teaching and research. Adoptees, I write this to empower you to see this guide as your own. For those who aren't adopted but want to be allies to adoptees, I write this to give you a "guest lens" in an adoptee space. Read closely, here is what you will want to know:

If you were able to see the adoptee within each piece – to see their human face, spirit, and feelings – regardless of whether their words resonated with where you stand within the constellation of adoption, you read it how you were supposed to.

Adoptees, if you found universality in pieces that resonate with your experience or empathy for pieces that did not, you read this guide how you were supposed to. I (and others like me) work for an adoption world in which I won't have to wonder if people will approach a guide written for adoptees/by adoptees and ask, "Whose guide is this anyway?"

Adoptees, the families and friends that love us, we need an adoption where all will say that what adoptees write – like The Adoptee Survival Guide – is adoptee writing and that's why it has value.

Amanda H.L. Transue-Woolston, MSS, LSW is an author, speaker, psychotherapist, and social worker with a Bachelor's degree and a Master's degree in social work. Amanda has served the adoption and foster care communities through individual and family clinical work, group work, writing and presenting, and working for positive policy change. Her writing and presentations have reached broad audiences through multiple books, magazines, major news and radio interviews, and conferences, and she has engaged with legislators at the state and congressional levels on adoption policy. Amanda is probably best known for her personal blog, The Declassified Adoptee.

Cover Art by Carlynne Hershberger

Carlynne Hershberger is co-owner of Hershberger & Huff Studios in Ocala, Florida. She is also co-author of the book *Creative Colored Pencil Workshop* by FW Media. Her award winning work has been exhibited in juried exhibitions across the country. Carlynne is a late discovery step-parent adoptee and also a mother who lost her newborn child to adoption in 1980. She has been reunited with her daughter since 2002. She blogs about her experience and is currently working on a painting series about adoption called Silent Voices.

"Traveling Chameleon" by Jake Mumma

Jake Mumma lives in Dayton, Ohio with his wife and two kids. He is the owner of Sketch Monkey's Artist for Hire and Nothing Presents Productions. He does work from animations to illustrations to paintings and more. Jake has been forming his style over the past 25 years and is currently working to bring out a new series of uplifting and inspiring children's stories.

You can visit Jake at www.Nothingpresents.com or email him at sktchmnky@gmail.com.

Why a Chameleon?

by Paige Adams Strickland

Chameleons are interesting creatures.

So are adoptees.

They have a purpose in the balance of the universe and deserve fair treatment as a respected part of nature,

as do adoptees.

Chameleons have amazing survival skills when coping with their environments.

Same with adoptees.

Chameleons are generally quiet, peace-seeking and aim to blend in with their living situation,

just like adoptees.

Chameleons exist all over the world, and probably didn't originate in the United States. They were brought here a long time ago.

Yes, like some adoptees!

Do you know what a chameleon thinks about a lot of its day?

Do you know what adoptees often ponder in their lives?

One difference between chameleons and adopted people might be while these small, less assertive, self-sufficient beings might prefer to hide and avoid being noticed, many grown adoptees now believe that it's time for us to be acknowledged by the law and society in general. We believe the days of running and hiding are over.

Chameleons and adoptees are delicate but very cool souls!

CPSIA information can be obtained at www.ICGtesting.com
Printed in the USA
LVOW11s2047220515

439574LV00001B/232/P